Slipping into Darkness
Blinded by the Light

Melanie E. Lewis

Copyright © May 3, 2013 by Melanie E. Lewis
Published by Cast the First Stone Press — 2016

No part of this book may be reproduced or transmitted in any form or by an electronic or mechanical means, including photocopying, recording or by any information storage and retrieval system, without the express written permission of the publisher, except where permitted by law.

Information available at: melanieelewis.com

ISBN: 9780997372458

Cover art by Melanie E. Lewis, inspired by Karen Young

Book design by D. Bass

Contact Melanie at castthefirststone1@gmail.com

Library of Congress Cataloging-in-Publication Data
Lewis, Melanie E.
1. Memoir 2. Drug addiction 3. Child abuse 4. Spirituality 5. Domestic violence 6. Christianity 7. LGBT 8. Relationships 9. Hepatitis C

Dedication

I dedicate this work to all the babies whose childhoods were stolen by circumstances beyond their control. May God bless and keep you.

A Note From the Author

Many thanks for taking time out of your life to allow me to share with you some of the times of my life. I have tried to be as honest as possible and as accurate as memory will permit. To protect the innocent and not so innocent, some of the names of the people you will meet during this sojourn with me have been changed. If I have offended anyone, please forgive me-that was never my intention.

Table of Contents

Acknowledgments	1
Intro to Hell	3
Getting High	23
Breaking Out	31
The Beasts	45
The Greatest Losses	57
Motherhood and Reconciliation	75
All You Need is Love	85
Gay and Godly	97
Peace	115
Companions and Contractors	123
Samantha	135
The Healing Continues	149
Boating and Betrayal	165
Stranded	179
Relationships	195
Meanderings	203
Never Alone	215
About the Author	223

ACKNOWLEDGEMENTS

To Monique and Laura, my lifelines in the wilderness. Thank you for your attentive ears, your supportive words and your loving hearts.

To Karen C., one of the kindest people I have ever met. Your time, guidance and encouragement in helping to bring this work to fruition will never be forgotten and always appreciated.

To my mother, without whom, I would have no life. Thank you for doing your very best. Miss you Mommy.

All glory to God, who gave me the words and graced me the time to grow up.

Biblical quotes are from NIV versions of the Bible.

INTRO TO HELL

Everybody leaves! Whether they walk, run, fly, or die, eventually and inevitably every relationship comes to an end. No one remains forever. My mother left on the 18th of February 1985. Her last words to me were, "Please don't hurt me." Mommy had been diagnosed with lung cancer shortly after she turned fifty years of age and departed six months later. The afternoon of her death was an egregiously sunny, frigid afternoon. Though there is much that escapes my memory about that day, about my life, I will never forget that unforgiving sun as it forbade my sleep while I lay curled up on my grandmother's couch, hung over from the night before, "babysitting" my mother.

Mama, (my grandmother) insisted on caring for Mommy after she was released from the hospital. I assumed she would live with me, as her well being always seemed to be my self-appointed responsibility. With ample space in my apartment, I planned to hire an aide to care for her during the day. But Mama was selfless, loving and wise—the very sinew of our family. "Thelma will stay with me," she declared, and that was that. So, my mother occupied one side of my grandparents' queen-sized bed, Papa (my grandfather), the other side.

Papa had Alzheimer's since the early 1970s, before it even had a name. Mama bathed, dressed, and fed him every day with love and tenderness, never a complaint. Come to think about it, where did Mama sleep, perhaps on the very couch where, this particular day, I could get no rest? I don't know. It never occurred to me to ask during any of my infrequent visits. Not that I didn't love my mother, on the contrary, I had been lovingly devoted to her all my life. Nor was I in denial. It was acutely evident that my mother was dying. In fact, when my mother was initially hospitalized, I was the first one to be advised of her diagnosis, inoperable metastatic cancer. After informing my family of her condition, I suggested we all meet at the hospital that night; however, I did not go to the hospital; instead, I stayed home and smoked cigarettes and drank cognac.

No, there was no denial. Maybe I was just undeniably pissed off that Mommy was abandoning me yet again, only this time forever, and there was so much unsaid.

That day, the day of my mother's departure, Mama had asked me to come and stay with Mommy while she and my aunt went to visit Papa, who had recently been hospitalized. There was nothing my grandmother could ask of me that I would not do for her. She was my heart. And after all, that was my mother lying there, dying. Though regrettably at the time, I was not accepting it graciously. So that day, I lay on the living room couch, twisting and turning, desperately trying to sleep, periodically checking on my mother. She was at a stage in her illness where she didn't speak much, at least not to me. She didn't appear to be in pain. She must have eaten occasionally. She just lay there, waiting, maybe thinking or praying, remembering or regretting, only God knows.

Our last conversation remains vivid in my memory. I had dragged myself from the couch to check on her and agonizingly, reluctantly began to change her diaper. Never in a million years did I think that...anyway, as gently and mindlessly as possible, I proceeded. My mother, with her frail body and her bald head, looked up at me, her big brown eyes wide open with fear. Despite all the damage she had endured, the cancer, the cancer treatments and the years of abuse, through all the pain, her beautiful face prevailed.

"Please don't hurt me." Her words cut to the quick of my soul.

Please don't hurt me. Did she say those words to my stepfather when he regularly beat her to a pulp while I helplessly, hopelessly watched, sometimes crying, screaming for him to stop, sometimes paralyzed in utter fear? Please don't HURT me! How could she say this to me? Had she realized how much she had hurt *me*, and how her life decisions had almost destroyed me? But perhaps she sensed the anger and betrayal I felt. An anger and betrayal, which I had not yet acknowledged because I couldn't allow myself to be aware of these feelings while my mother was still alive.

From the moment my mother told me that she was marrying Hollis Scott, my sole purpose in life became protecting her and trying to appease "Daddy." I was five years old. He hadn't shown his ugly side yet, but my *spirit* revealed to me that it was there. I remember looking in the mirror, talking to myself, and making the decision to call Hollis, Daddy. "Maybe that will make him be nice," I naively thought.

Hollis, a very handsome man, had dark brown skin with jet-black, wavy hair, a moustache and goatee. Mommy was fair-skinned, stylish, and very attractive. They made an incredibly striking couple.

I didn't attend the wedding. I recall lying on the bottom bunk bed in my grandparents' home, staring at the mattress above. Mommy, Aunt Joan, and I shared a room. Mommy was sitting on the edge of the bed in her beautiful white lace gown. "Melanie, baby, please, let's put on your pretty dress," she pleaded.

"No Mommy, I have a headache." I fought to hold back

my tears. Mommy had tears in her eyes, also. I just wanted her to go, just wanted to be alone. Little did I know, I was to feel alone for many years to follow. Although she continued to plead with me, I was having no part of that fiasco. If I could see it was a mistake at five, why couldn't she see it at twenty-five?

Mommy and me

Shortly after the wedding, Mommy and Hollis left for their honeymoon. Funny, a few years ago, my cousin sent me a video of the wedding, and no one looked happy, not Mommy or Hollis or Mama or Papa, not one smile. Hollis was from Trinidad, and that's where they went for their honeymoon, where he took her passport and kept her captive for six months. The beatings began there. I was too young to know what was going on, and Mama and Papa, wisely, did not discuss grown-up affairs in front of me. Years later, my mother informed me of the disturbing details.

When Mommy and Hollis finally returned to New York,

Wedding - Hollis & Manny

they lived in a room in Brooklyn. I visited them once. I must have been about six by then. We watched a movie on their small black and white television about a man who had just been run over by a car. I remember the horror of seeing this man lying in the street with his brains hanging out. This paled in comparison to the greater horror of seeing Hollis beating my mother, which somehow, for some reason, happened shortly afterwards. I never visited them in Brooklyn again, which was probably Hollis's goal.

Within the year they moved back to Staten Island, and I went to live with them. I wonder how many beatings Mommy took to persuade Hollis to agree to that.

Papa wanted me to live with him and Mama, but Mama said, "She's Thelma's child, she should be with her mother." So, off I went into Hollis Hell. Mommy was pregnant with my brother, Clifford. We lived in a two bedroom apartment in a two family house owned by the Fultons, a Black family. Mr. Fulton was a fireman, and his wife, Susie, was the consummate Southern housewife. They had five children, one of whom was my age. They were a good, solid, upstanding family, and there was a certain sense of security knowing they were right upstairs, especially when the screaming started. Eventually Mr. Fulton would knock on the door and make the beatings stop. He became my hero.

There was an incident during Mommy's pregnancy with Cliff. She must have been pretty far along as her belly was quite big. Hollis had come home from work, and they were in their bedroom talking. It didn't take long for the talking to escalate to yelling. Mommy came out of the room, walked into the kitchen and Hollis silently followed. I was on the couch in the living room, which was situated between their bedroom and the kitchen. I lost sight of them for a moment when they entered the kitchen, until I saw my mother's body flung into the refrigerator, which was near the kitchen entrance door. Hollis had her pinned against the side of the refrigerator as his battering fists rolled from her pregnant belly up to her face in a continual motion. His rage even exceeded his love for his unborn child.

A year after Cliff was born, my sister Carla came into the world. We all slept in one bedroom. Cliff and Carla in a crib and me on a bunk bed. We lived at the Fultons' for a few years. During that time, Hollis's mother came to visit us. She was a small built, dark brown woman with straight black hair, a big belly (she was not pregnant, at least not with child) and a huge lump behind her left ear that she would rub and then let out a long, beastly belch. She was scary—a witch. Every morning, she would get on her knees in our bedroom and chant. I would lie in bed watching her, trying to rebuke whatever demons she might be summoning. During her time with us, which seemed like months, my mother's hands and arms broke out in boils. They were so bad she had to soak them in some pungent smelling, purple solution and afterwards wear white gloves over her cracked, raw, weeping hands. That went on for months. Eventually, ghastly granny left, Mommy's hands cleared up and it was business as usual in Hollis's household.

After a few years with the Fultons we rented a house of our own, in the same town, Port Richmond, on Staten Island. I dreaded the move, as it meant there would be no Mr. Fulton to knock on the door and stop the beatings, no one around to hear our screams, no semblance of security. When we moved, a seed of panic rooted itself in my soul and never left.

Life in our new home on Harrison Avenue was trepidatious, to say the least. My mother worked hard at maintaining her marriage. She cooked three meals a day and always kept herself looking desirable. The house was clean, the children, well groomed, although I remember one day going to school in a skirt that had gum stuck on the back from a previous wearing. It was quite humiliating and hurtful to discover that I had walked around all day with a wad of gum on my rear. Why didn't she notice? I always knew my mother was preoccupied with making her marriage work, as if she had something to prove so I always tried to be as self-sufficient and as independent as possible. After all, my mother had enough on her plate, so I took myself off the menu. I didn't want to put any additional demands or stresses on Mommy.

I was intelligent enough to do my homework independently and was a pretty good student, all things considered. Books and music provided solace when I wasn't hanging out with friends. I started to use the term, "playing with friends," but, in actuality, by the age of eleven, I was already smoking cigarettes and drinking, so one could hardly consider that play.

Anyway, the fights continued although they shouldn't really be called fights because Mommy never physically defended herself. Beatings would be a more accurate description. It got to a point that I could tell when they were going to fight. Sometimes, during the day Mommy would play jazz recordings. The album *Desafinado* by Stan Getz was her favorite. I don't know if the music made her reminiscent of happier times, but *Desafinado* was an indicator. Alcohol, though, was a most definite indicator. If they both were drinking, or if Hollis went out to the bar and stayed too late, most times, it was fight night.

On Harrison Avenue no one came to stop Hollis. My brother, sister and I would look on, terrified, crying, screaming, begging him to stop. But that did not move him. Sometimes, I could tell when my mother was talking too much, arguing or goading him in some way—prelude to a beating. I would scream, "Mommy, shut up please!" But she would just continue. And inevitably the beating would ensue. Occasionally, someone would call the police, but domestic violence wasn't such a big thing back then in the sixties, especially not in a Black household. A couple of White cops would come, talk to Hollis on the porch and tell him to take a walk and cool off, and that would be the extent of their intervention. There were no arrests, no offer to take my mother to safe surroundings or even to the hospital. No help, just despair.

Even the men in my family rarely challenged him, not even when Hollis hit her right in front of them. The only one I ever saw unmoved by Hollis was Mama. I remember one night at Mama and Papa's house (Iris and Clifford were their names.) Mama and Mommy were sitting on the couch and Hollis was standing, facing them. Papa was standing to Hollis's far right, and I stood to his left. I don't remember what preceded this scene, but I do remember Hollis looming over Mommy and Mama. He raised his right leg to kick at them. Mommy seemed a bit fearful, but Mama sat there defiantly, with her arms crossed, without blinking an eye. Papa and I just stood there and looked on, without saying a word. Hollis, wearing pointy black leather shoes, kicked out again, and this time, he hit Mama in the face, around her eye. I was waiting for Papa to punch him in the face, but it didn't happen. Instead, Papa calmly approached Hollis to talk to him. Talk! It seemed hopeless. Would no one vanquish this monster?

Our home was a comfortable and seemingly inviting two-story house. Of our immediate family—Mama, Papa and their other two daughters, Barbara and Joan, and their families—we were the only ones living in a house with a backyard and a pool. The bedrooms were located upstairs. There were two regular sized bedrooms and a tiny room with a slanted ceiling located just off the stairs. Initially, Cliff,

Carla, and I all shared the second bedroom. However, as I was older, I wanted some privacy, so I moved into the tiny room with the slanted ceiling. Although there was more privacy from my brother and sister, unfortunately, I could hear the goings on in my parents' bedroom more clearly.

There were times I really hated Hollis. I'd lie awake some nights plotting to stab him in the heart while he slept. But I was always afraid that he would wake up or that I wouldn't completely kill him, and then he would kill me, or I would be sent to jail and Mommy would be alone. So we all just endured. Though I knew why I was staying, I couldn't understand why Mommy stayed.

Years later, my mother told me the story of her romance with my biological father, Arthur, which helped me to understand her marriage to Hollis. Arthur was married to another woman when he and my mother met. As the story goes, his wife (who was a nurse) had become pregnant while she and my father were just dating. He encouraged her to have an abortion, which left her sterile. He then felt obligated to marry her. Years later he and Mommy met and fell in love. Then came me. My father ran the usual married man line, "I'm going to leave my wife as soon as..." And then, a few years after I was born, his wife miraculously got pregnant and gave birth to a baby girl. Well, my father, "honorable" man that he was, was then compelled to stay with his wife. After all, she had more education than my mother, she was his wife, and he had a reputation to uphold, et cetera, et cetera. Sadly, until he died at the age of fifty-three, my father remained unhappily married to his wife, drinking scotch most of his days and spending many of his nights with random women. I surmised that my mother married Hollis Scott out of hurt, feelings of rejection, and perhaps a little spite.

I recall being overjoyed whenever we had company because then *Scotty* would emerge. (Scotty is what Hollis's clueless casual acquaintances called him, way too innocuous a name for such a bastard). Everyone thought Scotty was such a great guy. Those lumps, bruises and black eyes? No! Not Scotty. Thelma must have fallen down some stairs or something. In the latter years, Hollis started displaying his violent temper even when we had visitors. I think it's true what they say about bullies, though. You know, about standing up to them. I remember one afternoon when my mother had gone to visit Mama. Mommy had just taken a job, her first one since her marriage because Hollis forbade her to work. I was home alone. As I sat in the living room watching TV, Hollis came in and walked past me without saying a word. He went upstairs to their bedroom. I sensed something was amiss, so I went upstairs to my room, pretending to look for something. As I passed their bedroom, I saw that he had taken all my mother's clothing out of the closet. I surreptitiously spied on him from my room. He sat on the side of their bed and calmly, almost emotionlessly, began to shred every stitch of Mommy's clothing with a straight razor. Oh boy, this was serious. I went downstairs and called my mother to tell her what he was doing. I begged her not to come home.

"But I have to come home," was her reply.

Hollis only beat me once during their marriage. This occurred when I was eleven or twelve. I don't recall whether it was before or after the clothing shredding incident, but in retrospect it makes more sense that it would have happened before. The night of my beating, he had come home from Buddy's bar, the neighborhood pool hall on the corner, full of Schaefer beer. It was shortly after 9 p.m. My mother and I were watching television. He asked me what I was doing up. I respectfully replied, "Mommy said I could stay up and watch TV." "What time did I tell you to go to bed?" Timidly, I answered, "nine o'clock."

He went to the basement and returned with a rubber extension cord, then pulled me upstairs and whipped me, right in the center of their bedroom. I tried to keep my cries to a minimum while he beat me, knowing that he was trying to provoke my mother so he could beat her too. Throughout the marriage I always felt I was my mother's protector, even though there was little I could do. I could be there for her, if only to bring her ice for her busted lips and battered face, or some tissue to help wipe away her tears. I could be there to pretend I didn't see the shame in her blackened eyes or hear the hopelessness in her voice. That's why when my biological father asked me years earlier if I wanted to live with him I told him, "No, I need to be here for Mommy." She did eventually come upstairs the night Hollis beat me, and I think she did get her beating that night, too. I don't really remember. That was the only beating (or spanking) I ever got in my life. I was a good kid, until I wasn't.

I would like to believe that night inspired my mother to start standing up to him, despite what she thought she had to prove to herself, or to my father, or to the world. So, Mommy came home that day, the day of the shredding of the clothing, and Hollis descended from his little tower of terror and got in her face. They were in the kitchen. *We* were in the kitchen. I don't remember what he said, what justification with which he was trying to qualify the impending beating, but I clearly remember my mother that day. She looked as beautiful as ever. Her big brown eyes meticulously accented with mascara and eyebrow pencil. Her auburn hair dyed to compliment her fair, perfect, dark ivory complexion and her nails manicured and polished (Mommy did all this herself.) Always well dressed, my mother had innate class and style. She looked good no matter what she was wearing. Her beauty and femininity were to her, her greatest and most important attributes. Her favorite compliment was that she looked like Elizabeth Taylor, which she did.

Anyway, Hollis was well into his rant. I'll never forget the look on Mommy's face. She was fearless. My mother stood there in the kitchen, calmly stared him in the eyes, folded her arms across her chest, and proclaimed: "One of us is going to die today. I don't know who it will be, but ONE of us is going to die TODAY!" I wish I had seen the expression on Hollis's face, but I was too mesmerized by my mother. Now, this is the Thelma I knew and loved, that look of resolute determination in her eyes. She had had ENOUGH! Mommy was going to fight back this time.

It reminded me of an incident when I was about four or five. Mommy and I still lived with Mama and Papa in the Berry Houses, the whitest housing project in New York City, at least back then, so it was before she married Hollis. I was playing in the lobby of our building, proudly donning my new cowboy hat and holster with two silver six-shooters. Sometimes for fun the neighborhood kids would "stick the elevator." What we would do is after someone got in the elevator, just as the elevator door was closing we would pull the elevator entrance door and the elevator wouldn't go anywhere.

This boy I knew from the neighborhood, Billy, a ten-year-old, freckly-faced Irish kid, got in the elevator. I playfully ran over and pulled the door so it would stick. Billy pressed the button for his floor again, I again ran over and pulled the door, and then, giggling, ran back to the entrance of the building. Billy opened the elevator door and yelled, "Cut it out!" Silly little girl that I was, I did it one more time. It must have pissed Billy off because he got off the elevator and angrily walked toward me. His aggression frightened me, so I pulled my gun from its holster and popped him in the forehead with the butt of it and then ran upstairs to our apartment. Mommy was bathing, getting ready to go to work. I sat on the living room couch, anxiously awaiting the repercussions of my actions.

Shortly afterwards the doorbell rang. Mommy was out of the tub by then, in her underwear. She slipped on a robe and went to the door. I apprehensively followed. It was Billy's mother, a squat, stout, pie-faced woman with limp hair and freckles like Billy. She was angrily recounting the episode between Billy and me and ended with the statement, "I told him not to play with niggers." She turned and walked toward the elevator. Mommy didn't say a word. She finished putting on her uniform, combed her hair, gently took my hand and said, "Come on, Melanie." We got on the elevator and went up to the fifth floor where Billy lived. Mommy rang the bell. When Billy's mom opened the door, BAM! My mother punched her right in her face. She then took my hand again and we returned to our apartment.

Well, Hollis backed the hell up real quick that day, the day of the clothing shredding. There were no beatings that day. My mother did start working after the standoff in the kitchen and Hollis Scott left shortly afterwards, for good. I still remember his last words. He was at the front door. It was the day before my brother's seventh birthday. Little Cliff anxiously asked, "Daddy are you going to get cake and ice cream for my birthday tomorrow?" Hollis hesitated at the front door, turned, looked at my mother and said, "That used to be." Cliff's little head just fell along with his heart. And that was the end of Hollis Scott in my life.

If Hollis beating me helped to empower my mother, then those were the best scars I've ever gotten. Sometimes we don't have enough love for ourselves to overcome ourselves, if you know what I mean. Sometimes it takes a greater love, like the love for your child, to inspire us to do better, despite our fears or insecurities. I'd like to believe my mother's love for me inspired and encouraged her. I don't know.

Intro to Hell

We really didn't discuss Hollis after he left. He never paid any child support or helped my mother financially in any way. He never visited his children. After Hollis left, Mommy took care of us by herself and very well I might add. She worked as a nurse's aide in a nursing home. Not such a glamorous career for so beautiful a woman, changing old people's diapers, bathing and dressing them. But she did her job with grace, kindness, and with dignity, and never a complaint. She even helped to fund my first year in physical therapy school. Without her help, I may not have become a physical therapist at all.

Mommy remained married to Hollis for eight years. Eight years of merciless beatings whenever it struck his fancy. Eight years of my mother appeasing him in every way, trying to be a good wife. Eight years of me living in fear, desperation and isolation. No wonder by the time he left I was well on my way to becoming a heroin addict. But I forgive him, for everything.

And hey, don't feel too sorry for me concerning my one beating. I got my licks in too. When I was eight years old, Hollis caught the mumps from me and became sterile. So basically, according to the Caribbean mentality I took his manhood. Now, that I think about it, he must have been waiting for years to find an excuse to beat me.

Funny thing though, one sleepless night, during the writing of this book, I began to remember so much more about my relationship with Hollis. My mind drifted to the fishing trip I had planned for the next day, which prompted me to recall how I learned to fish: Hollis taught me. I thought about our family outings. Mommy would pack up some sandwiches and Kool-aid, and we would all pile into our Chevy station wagon and off we would go to Great Kills or Midland Beach. We basically caught two kinds of fish, bluefish and flukes. Bluefish are a medium sized, greasy kind of fish with dark flesh. The fluke is a flat fish. One side is green and has two eyes, one above the other. The other side is white and plain and smooth. Hollis taught me how to bait a hook with sandworms. They were fat and green and could actually bite you with their pincers if you weren't careful. Hollis even took me deep sea fishing once, just the two of us on a charter trip. He took me to work with him, again, just Hollis and me. He was a laboratory technologist. He taught me to see through a microscope, something that so impressed me, I even considered studying laboratory technology in college.

That night my mind was flooded with countless pleasant childhood memories. We would go to the drive-in theater, the entire family: Hollis, Mommy, Cliff, Carla and I. Sometimes, we would eat out at Wetson's, a McDonalds predecessor. Hollis took me bowling with him, again, just him and me. He was in a bowling league. When we got to the alley, he would bowl a game with me before he began bowling with his teammates. Afterwards, he would give me money to buy hot chocolate and cookies from the vending machine. That was my favorite part.

Our Christmas tree was never without an abundance of gifts, and I always got at least one major item I was hoping for. So... Perhaps Hollis wasn't as monstrous as I have chosen to remember all these years. It seemed that I had been looking at him through a microscope. I wonder why it is that the mistakes, the wrongdoings, the weaknesses of those with whom we are in relationship too often negate the good they have shared with us and done for us. Hollis even inadvertently protected me from continued molestation by my grandmother (my father's mother, Agatha) and her husband, Mr. Thompson, by forbidding me to have any contact with my father and his parents. I've forgiven them, too. Agatha and her husband, that is, though, I can't say I hope they are resting in peace. I never discussed it with my mother, regrettably one of the unsaids.

Truth is, Hollis taught me some good things, valuable things that would stay with me throughout my life. He spent quality time with me and must have said some nice things from time to time—encouraging words, loving words. Yet all I could clearly recall him saying is, "What time did I tell you to go to bed?" His hands must have done some good works. He fed me, he clothed me, and did fun things with me. But all that stood out in my memory these many years were the beating fists.

Wow, I gotta tell you! That night, when I started thinking about fishing, just lying there in my bed in the Bahamas, unable to sleep, I discovered a deeper forgiveness for Hollis and a love, I had never acknowledged before in my life for Hollis...Scotty...Daddy. Maybe Mommy truly loved him. Maybe that's why she stayed.

And now my mother lies here dying. Her last words to me will be, "Please don't hurt me." With tears in my eyes, I was barely able to utter my reply, "Mommy, I don't want to hurt you. I'm just trying to make you more comfortable." I would like to say that I kissed her or even sat with her and held her hand, but I didn't—one of my great regrets. Instead, I finished changing her diaper and went back to the couch, futilely trying to shield my eyes from that damn bright winter sun, so I could just get some rest. The next time I checked on her, she was gone.

Upon discovering my mother's lifeless body, I called my brother, who told me to call 911. I did so, against my better judgment. I knew I should have left Mommy in peace. But I was haunted by the incontrovertible fact that we didn't even get the chance to say good-bye or to say I love you. Had I ever told my mother that I loved her, actually said the words?

EMS came and performed the whole resuscitation procedure, injecting her with needles, shocking her with defibrillator paddles, all the while chatting and laughing amongst themselves about things unrelated to my dead mother. I was horrified and ashamed of myself for letting these people touch and disturb her. When they left, needle wrappers and other medical paraphernalia littered the floor of Mama's bedroom. With my mother's body disheveled and disrespected, I couldn't bear to look at her. Cliff came shortly after. Before Mama and Aunt Joan returned, we cleaned up the refuse the EMS team had left behind and replaced the covers on Mommy's body. How I wish I had lain with her and held her, comforted her and been there for her during her last hours. Ever since I can remember, from the age of five, I had been there for her. Yet at the very end, for the last six months of her life, I abandoned her. What must she have thought of me?

We didn't have many meaningful conversations after her hospitalization. I do remember a visit to the hospital at Christmas time. I had invited the family to Mommy's room to celebrate the holiday with her. She had on a blue robe, the same color and style Cliff would wear seven years later. She was sitting on her bed, and while the rest of us all flitted around, trying to make merry, my eyes suddenly caught hers, and in them all I saw was anger and disappointment. Perhaps she didn't feel like being around a lot of folks, even family. Or maybe she was angry with her illness, or the cigarette companies, or herself, or maybe even God. Possibly, she already felt abandoned by me. I don't know. As I said, I don't recall we ever spoke from the heart once she got ill.

Before she died, she did tell me she loved me in a thank you note. "Dear Baby, I cannot find the words to say how surprised I was or how much I appreciate the wonderful birthday party you gave me. Except to say I love you and I thank you for being a beautiful daughter. Love, Mommy." It is dated 6/84. It was her 50th birthday. We never suspected

Mommy's Birthday Party

it would be her last.

Later that evening, the evening of my mother's death I went into my grandmother's kitchen cabinet for something and discovered my mother's morphine tablets. I picked one up and stared at it, remembering how wonderful a heroin high used to be. There was a time when I swore I would never stop shooting dope. Heroin filled me with a warm sensation that started in my throat and slowly spread throughout my body, covering me in a blanket of security and oblivion. There is absolutely nothing like it. Oh, to be able to feel that just once again, especially now. It couldn't be more justified. There were quite a few tablets left there, in Mama's kitchen cabinet. They wouldn't be missed. I could say I threw them down the incinerator, yeah, to remove temptation from my brother Cliff, who was having his own drug issues at the time. But I would have so very much to lose. That is, if I let things get out of control.

GETTING HIGH

I first shot dope at the age of thirteen. My friends were already "shooting up." Because I was the youngest in the group, they all tried to protect me, only allowing me to sniff the dope, until I convinced them that I could handle shooting it just as well as they did. It seems unimaginable now, a baby sticking needles into her veins to get "high." Back in the late sixties, however, drugs were very prevalent. I used all kinds of illegal substances: LSD, mescaline, reefer (as we called it then), amphetamines, barbiturates, anything to just get away, to ease the pain that I wasn't even aware existed. I was just getting high, like everyone else.

Heroin became my drug of choice. It was so good at easing that pain. I shot dope for about two years. One usually begins by skin-popping, injecting the heroin into your thigh. Mainlining (injecting directly into your veins) is the next progression as one desires to feel the effect quicker and more intensely. It didn't take me long to advance to that next step. Mainlining left telltale signs, called track marks, which developed when you injected yourself in the same area of the same vein over and over. Eventually a scar would develop over the length of the most frequented vein. My mother didn't seem to notice until I overdosed one night.

After Hollis left, we moved from Harrison Avenue to what was then a kind of luxury apartment in Fox Hill on Staten

Island. My French tutor, a handsome, young White journalist, had developed an affinity for my family and helped Mommy get the apartment. I was dealing heroin for this guy, Jerry, who lived in my building. I had a dealing partner, J.R., but all the drugs were stashed in my room. The day of my overdose, J.R. called up to my bedroom window at the front of the building. I went to the window, but my mother was standing behind me, not visible to J.R. He yelled up to me, "Hey, Mel, throw down the stuff!"

I gave him a queer look. "What are you talking about?"

"Throw down the stuff!" he repeated.

"Look, man, I'll be out in a little while. I'll talk to you later."

When a dope fiend wants to get high, he or she wants to get high immediately. Before I could walk away from the window, J.R. yells out, "Throw down the dope!" At that moment my mother jumped to the window and almost through it, cursing out J.R. and running him off. J.R. had been infected with the polio virus as a child, so he wasn't running very quickly, but he sure did hop down the street in record time.

Mommy then demanded that I turn the drugs over to her. Back then, heroin was packaged in glassine bags that sold for five dollars a piece. I had two half loads of heroin—about thirty bags. My mother took the drugs and growled, "Well, I'm flushing this garbage right down the toilet!"—a fate I apparently narrowly escaped as a fetus. Later that day, my mother informed me that she should have flushed *me* down the toilet when she had the chance.

"Ma, those drugs aren't mine, but you do what you think you need to do."

Shortly afterwards, Jerry (the dealer), J.R., and some other shady characters gathered in front of the building, obviously conspiring as to how to get their dope. My mother opened the door to my room with the dope in her hand, concern on her face, and fear in her voice. She told me, "Here, take this downstairs and give it to them, and get your ass right back up here."

I put the dope in my pocket and went downstairs.

"J.R., what the hell is wrong with you man? Couldn't you tell that I couldn't talk? Now the dope is gone! My mother flushed it down the toilet. Sorry Jerry, but J.R. blew it man. And now I'm on punishment, so I have to go back upstairs, sorry man." No one saw my smile when I turned and walked away.

Jerry was speechless. I guess he'll think twice before having a fourteen-year-old deal for him again. At that time on Staten Island the dope dealers weren't very ruthless, so I could get away with pulling a stunt like that, at least once. Anyway, I skipped back upstairs with thirty bags of dope in my pocket. Thanks Mom!

That evening my mother, brother, and sister went to Mama's house. I was alone with my unsavory stash. I had my own bedroom, which was nicely furnished with a stereo cassette player that my father, Arthur, had bought me for Christmas. There was also a TV, posters, and all types of hippie and drug paraphernalia that were so popular back then. I was the hippie of my group of friends, with my tie-dyed jeans, peace sign medallion, rock music and all. My room was the hangout, a great place to get high because my mother worked nights while I babysat my brother and sister. But this night she wasn't at work, and I was alone. This night, I chose not to hang out and get high in my most groovy room. Inexplicably, instead, I chose to go into my brother and sister's room. Their bunk beds had been stripped of their linens. I remember climbing to the top bunk with my works (the term used for the needle and the cooker, usually a bottle cap or a teaspoon), a belt to tie up my arm so that my veins would be more prominent, and the rest of the equipage required to shoot up heroin. In the cooker was a tiny wad of cotton to filter out the impurities. I would draw the prized potion up the hypodermic needle through the cotton ball. Little did I suspect or care that more deadly diseases unfilterable by the little cotton ball may have been present.

I also needed matches to heat the mixture of heroin and water and to light a cigarette immediately after I shot up. You think a cigarette is good with a cup of coffee? Try one after a shot of heroin! There is nothing like nodding out, pain-free with your cigarette dangling from your fingertips without ever dropping it. I've seen some folks actually continue to nod without so much as a flinch, while their cigarette burnt the flesh away between the two fingers from which it was dangling. Now *that's* pain-free.

So, that night I climbed to the top bunk with my works, my dope, and my cigarettes, sat on the bare mattress, and proceeded to get high. (To this day, I don't know why I went into that room.) When I awakened the next morning, the needle was still hanging from my forearm. Dried blood made a line down my arm with a pooled drop at the end, like a big, red teardrop. I didn't smoke any cigarettes that night and I didn't nod out. No, instead I killed myself. But my Heavenly Father showed me the love and the mercy to wake me up the next morning.

Well, I think that day, the day after I overdosed, the day I spent on my knees in front of the toilet, vomiting out the poison I had injected myself with the previous night, that day, my mother finally had to acknowledge my need for some attention.

A few days later, I got kicked out of high school. When I kept nodding out in one of my classes, the teacher sent me to the principal's office. While I sat there he looked at me with pity and disdain all in one stare. He took my left arm in his hand, outstretched it before me, and pointing to the fresh needle marks, he asked, "What is this on your arm?"

I didn't bother to explain that they were the tracks of my tears. Instead, I merely answered, "I don't know."

"Well, God didn't put them there," he replied as he picked up the phone to call my mother.

Unable to live in denial any longer, Mommy began seeking the help for me that I so clearly and desperately needed. My father was the Assistant District Attorney. All he did, though, was inform me each time he convicted one of my acquaintances for drug possession. I guess he was trying to scare me straight, but it didn't work, and it wasn't helpful.

I interviewed at Daytop Village, but they didn't accept me. Perhaps I didn't seem like a viable candidate because I really wasn't ready to stop getting high. So with the help of my Uncle Dan, who was a social worker, I was admitted into Phoenix House. I will always be grateful to him for helping to save my life. At the tender age of fourteen I was living with hardcore convicts who had opted out of prison by going into rehab. I was living with recovering longtime drug addicts, women and men. Women who had prostituted themselves for the love of the drug. Women who had scars on their arms and legs, not only track marks but also big holes where they had developed abscesses from putting shared, disease ridden needles into the same scar over and over again until it became infected and couldn't heal. Women who had abandoned their children to get high; who had spent years in prison; who lied, cheated, stole, and lost jobs, family, and friends. Funny how *low* one will go to get *high*. Women just like me, trying to ease the pain that they didn't know they had or were too ashamed to acknowledge.

I was admitted into Phoenix House in 1968 when the average stay in a rehab center was about eighteen months. Now, unfortunately, I think it's about three to six months.

The first thirty days are spent in what they called induction, during which time one was not allowed any contact with their former life. No phone calls, letters, no outside contact at all. Following induction I was transferred to my permanent house. Back then there were Phoenix Houses in all five boroughs of New York. I went to Far Rockaway, Queens to a giant green and white house that looked like a big, old castle, located a block from the beach. It was the perfect place for my rehabilitation, close to the ocean. There were about seventy or so residents in our house, our ages ranging from nine to sixty-nine. Yes, little Randy, who probably shot more dope than I, was only nine. Wonder what he went through in his short life to be driven to putting needles in his arm.

Phoenix House was very structured. The house was run by Phoenix House graduates. The residents performed all the necessary duties to maintain the house. Everyone had a job. The service crew, entry-level position, cleaned the house. The kitchen crew prepared the meals. The expeditors policed. There were administrative offices, an acquisition department that procured donations, and even a legal department, all run by residents. It was just like the real work world. We got up at a certain time. We shared meals at scheduled times. We lived in rooms with two or three other residents and slept in bunk beds. We were responsible for maintaining our rooms in a proper fashion, which the expeditors would check every morning from our dresser drawers to our floors and toilet. If we fell short in performing our chores there were consequences.

After breakfast, we would have morning meetings when all community announcements were made, including the "funk list" — the expeditors' reports of those individuals who fell short in performing their personal chores or hygienic responsibilities. We ended with residents volunteering to lead us in their favorite song. An upbeat version of "Ebb

Tide" was the house favorite, perhaps because we were near the ocean. More than a therapeutic community, we became like family to each other. And just like families, there was always some kind of discord. That's what our encounter groups were for. Three nights a week we were assigned to groups of about ten people. Each group was led by a staff member or older resident. If you wanted to confront someone, you would "drop a slip" on him or her with your concern, your name, and the name of the other person, so you would both be in the same group that night.

We weren't allowed to just randomly confront fellow residents at will. We were there to learn how to deal with our feelings. One of our most popular aphorisms was "It's only a feeling, it will go away." The encounter groups were where we explored our feelings. That's where one could curse, cry, and express any emotions, whether they were about other residents, yourself, your mother, your father, etc. As the months went by, my head gradually cleared. And as I listened and cried, and loved—I grew, and one thing became very evident to me: *We are all the same*—Black, White, old, young; it didn't matter. We were all the same. As the saying goes "We are more alike than we are different." Everyone has been hurt. Everyone wants love and acceptance. Finally, I was not ALONE! For the first time since I was five years old, I felt safe. I felt secure. I could breathe again without that root of panic strangling my lungs, making me gasp in pain for every breath. For the first time since I was five years old, I felt like I belonged.

Thank God my mother sent me back when two months into the program, I ran away. I was on the service crew, cleaning the assistant director's room and decided to climb down the fire escape and head for home. I tried to convince my mother that I was *all better* now and ready to come back. Fortunately, they had already called her and convinced her that I was indeed *not* all better. My mother cried most of that night as it grieved her to have to return me to Phoenix House, but return me she did the very next morning.

The frightening reality is that the entire time, sixteen months that I lived with these women and men in Phoenix House I continued to tell myself that when I got out, I was going to get high again because it just felt so good!

It wasn't until maybe a few weeks before I was scheduled to graduate from the program that I started seriously contemplating the consequences of getting high once more. For sixteen months someone had told me when to get up, when to go to bed, what to wear, what to eat, and where I could or could not go. I had no control of my own life. I had always been very independent, doing what I wanted to do, especially after Hollis left. Did I really want to risk my freedom again? Was heroin really that good? I decided it wasn't, thanks to God. And the night of my mother's death, when I held her morphine tablets in my hand and contemplated entertaining my pain, I decided NO once again.

And I poured myself a drink, instead.

BREAKING OUT

I graduated from Phoenix House in 1970 at the age of sixteen. A whole new crew of folks had moved into our apartment building. Heroin was pretty much out and cocaine was in. I didn't indulge too much in coke, only if someone was turning me on (getting me high for free) which was rare. Most times, my new friends and I smoked herb and drank cheap wine, like Boone's Farm Strawberry Field or Scuppernong, which was my favorite.

There were many programs for job training available back then. I began a program at Manufacturers Hanover Trust Bank, training to be a transcription typist, the most boring job you could ever imagine. There was a roomful of women at desks with headphones, listening to dictation and typing *all day long.* At the end of the day, you actually had to give a count of how many words you typed that day. Whew, who wouldn't need a joint after that? But that didn't last long. I knew I needed to further my education. So, having earned my High School Equivalency diploma while in Phoenix House, off to community college I went.

The years following my release from Phoenix House were good. Mommy, Cliff, Carla, and I lived in relative peace. I went to school, worked part-time, hung out with my friends in my free time, and basically lived my life, unencumbered by anyone or anything.

I was nineteen when I decided it was time to truly exercise my freedom as a human *being*. I have always loved music, especially love songs, always been in love with love, and always loved girls. When I was in Phoenix House they told me the reason I shot dope was because of my attraction to females. That was surely an inadequate and inaccurate explanation for my self-destructive behavior. During my stay there, I was forced to date boys. One of the assistant directors even went so far as to stipulate that I must lose my virginity before I could be released. Fortunately, that was rescinded by the director of the house.

Upon returning home, I tried to maintain a straight lifestyle and date guys. They were like buddies because my heart was just not into anything more. My boyfriends were good friends, so there was no ugly drama when things didn't go where they may have liked them to go. I kept up the façade more for my mother than for any other reason. She so valued femininity and beauty, neither of which qualities I possessed to any significant extent. What a disappointment I must have been to her in that regard. I would think of the lyrics to the Jimi Hendrix song, "If Six Was Nine," "I'm the one that's got to die when it comes time for me to die, so let me live my life, the way I want to." I decided to pursue my true heart's desire: women.

My first lesbian encounter was initiated through the personal ads of The Village Voice. Her name was Gwen. One day when we were talking on the phone, my mother must have overheard part of the conversation. When I finished, she called me into the living room. She sat on the couch and I stood across the room facing her.

"Melanie, do you like girls?" she asked sternly.

"Yes, Mommy, I do," I answered with an equal amount of conviction.

She began crying. "Why Melanie? *Why?* Oh God, what

have I done wrong?" As if it was all about her.

Once again, attempting to protect her, I reassuringly replied, "It's not about you Mommy, it's all me."

She wallowed in self-pity a few more minutes, but there was nothing more to say, so I dismissed myself. As we carried on with the day's activities, passing each other from time to time, I could feel my mother's eyes following me, trying to penetrate my very core. We encountered each other's eyes in the kitchen, hers filled with disappointment and disdain, mine, just determined.

Finally she said, "You're going to have to find some place to live. I can't stand to look at you any longer."

I calmly answered, "I've already started looking for an apartment." And indeed, I had.

Shortly after Mommy's painful words to me, I moved into my first apartment, a four story walk-up in the East Village of Manhattan. It was an old tenement building with a small bathtub in the kitchen. When my mother first saw my prospective new home, she begged me to continue to live with her. "You could save your money and buy a car," she argued. I kindly but adamantly declined. My apartment was fabulous to me, and I was FREE! I was not responsible for anyone but myself. I could do what I wanted to do and be who I wanted to be. It was the most liberating feeling I had ever experienced.

Not long after I was settled in, Mommy began to see just how fabulous it/I was. She had come over one day to visit. We walked around the Village, listened to the musicians in Washington Square Park, had some dinner, and just hung out. She loved it and would come to visit often. She was pleased and proud of the way I could so easily just hang and make a great day of it. But that was my life in the East Village.

Most of the days were easy and great, though busy and full. One day, I was taking a bath in the four foot long tub in my kitchen. My feet hung over the end of the tub, dangling above the kitchen sink. I was sipping a glass of Fuki plum wine, my personal favorite back then; it went well with herb (marijuana). Mommy smiled at me and said, "Only you could make bathing in a little tenement tub look elegant." That year she gave me my first set of crystal wine glasses for Christmas. Ironically, that apartment would become the last place my mother lived before she died. She would discover her freedom there also, only for it to be rapidly, savagely snatched away from her with a death sentence diagnosis.

I had some of the best times of my life during the years in that East Village tenement apartment. I worked full-time, went to school full-time, and partied full-time. It was a blast! I used to hang out at one of the most famous lesbian bars in New York, Bonnie & Clyde's. Following the Stonewall riots of 1969, the gay rights movement had begun to emerge. The violent protests against the New York Police Department's raid of the Stonewall Inn, a gay bar in Greenwich Village, had given way to the first gay pride marches in New York, Chicago, and Los Angeles in 1970, commemorating the anniversary of the Stonewall riots. Bonnie & Clyde's was also in Greenwich Village, as were most gay clubs in New York City at that time. My friend Beverli, whom I met in Phoenix House, introduced me to the club. She was straight, but she was like an older sister, and she knew Manhattan well.

When we arrived at the bar, I was stupefied. Was I really in a roomful of gay women? Women who liked women, just like me? I sat there, spellbound. As my brain slowly absorbed the reality of this wonderland of lesbians, I also noticed something rather disappointing. The room was filled with White dykes. There were very few women of color and no perceivably feminine women. My heart sank. Is this what I would have to choose from, masculine looking, unappealing women in plaid flannel shirts and Frye boots?

Glory Days

Fortunately, I later discovered the women of color hung out on Wednesday nights when there was no cover charge. We had gone on a Friday night. Well, as I was living in the East Village and working in the West Village, which was only a ten minute bike ride away, Bonnie & Clyde's became like a second home to me, to all of us lesbian girls. I was like a kid in a candy store, so many flavors. Some nights I would actually sit with my back to the bar, watching the women as they came in to see who would be the lucky girl that night. I was the lucky one. Lucky that AIDS wasn't running rampant through our community yet. AIDS didn't even have a name until the early 1980s. So, although I did have a few committed relationships during that time, I was pretty promiscuous.

Taking my first official girlfriend to meet my mother was quite an event. I was dressed in my liberation costume, black suede Lil' Abner boots, a long straight man tailored coat, and a Stetson-like hat. Lena was slim with a cute shape, a big Afro, and nice full lips. She tasted like strawberries. Lena and I were sitting on the couch, the same blue couch from which my mother had questioned my sexuality the previous year. Mommy sat a few feet away at the dining room table. She was having a drink, rum, scotch, or something along that order. She just sat there staring at us, not saying a word, looking away only to reach for her drink. She would look at us, then take a gulp, then look at us again, and take another gulp. This went on for I don't know how long, a look and a gulp.

Finally, Mommy got up from the table. She looked at us again, let out a long sigh, and collapsed on the floor. I rushed over to her and helped her to the bedroom. "Mommy, are you okay?" I wasn't seriously concerned, because I knew Mom could be a bit dramatic at times, especially when she drank. She looked me dead in the eyes and gasped, "She isn't even pretty!"

My mother gradually began to accept my lifestyle. She must have received some negative feedback from certain members of my family, however, because one day she said to me, "Don't worry about what anyone else has to say about you. As long as I accept you, that's all that matters." She never questioned my sexuality again. And no member of my family ever questioned me or had anything derogatory to say about my sexuality, at least not to my face.

I was about twenty-six when I decided it was time to completely rule out men as possible partners by sleeping with one, just to make sure I didn't want one. Who better than my friend Kurt? We had kissed in the past, and he always professed his love for me. I was attracted to him, and he would truly appreciate what was being given to him. I called him one night and told him I was coming over. He knew immediately what the deal was. We did it. He wanted me to spend the night so he could really express himself to me, but once was enough for me. I got the gist of it. I put on my clothes, wished him good-night, and headed back home to the East Village, believing that I, at least, had given men a chance. Many years later, he told me he cried that night. I called him my chick, and we laughed about it. It's good to have old friends.

After Kurt, I had a few one-night stands with men. Lust? Curiosity? I have difficulty accepting the label of homosexual, gay etc. LABELS ARE LIMITING! I will call myself a lesbian. The word lesbian being defined as a woman who loves other women. But I will not limit myself, my life, or my state of being, by proclaiming that I am *only* capable of loving women. Even now at the age of sixty, post menopausal, diminished libido, shrinking ovaries and all, I couldn't say that I completely rule out men although I haven't been with one in over twenty-five years. As I have never had a meaningful sexual/emotional relationship with a man in the past, it's highly unlikely that it's going to happen over the next thirty years or so. But you never know what life has to offer you.

I do know I love women. Why? Only God knows for sure. I've had many theories, but that's a whole other book. I've always loved psychology and the pursuit of understanding why we do the things we do and what makes us who we are.

Perhaps it's a purely egocentric pursuit on my behalf, my need to understand me, my desire for resolution, and to be at peace within myself. We all want peace, no?

While attending college, I considered becoming a laboratory technologist like Hollis. But during that time my cousin was born with cerebral palsy, and I started to hear about physical therapy, which ultimately became my field of study. My intentions were to help him and children like him. However, once I began to work in the field, I discovered that working in pediatrics was just too heart wrenching for me, so I focused more on acute care and geriatrics. Having always been a caretaker and problem solver, acute care allowed me to see the results of my work and was very fulfilling.

Geriatrics paid well and was fun. The elderly tend to be honest and appreciative of attention and affection. Most of them were in the nursing home to stay. They had worked hard all their lives, saved money, and made plans for life after retirement, only to have a stroke, or amputation, or some other chronic debilitating illness that would result in their banishment to the nursing home. There, they helplessly watched their money, plans, and very lives tragically expire. For most of them physical therapy was just an activity, a place to socialize and get a little attention and a little tender loving care. While I understood their hopelessness, I tried to be motivating and do as much clinically as could be done. But in my heart I knew that sometimes just loving them was therapy enough.

I do have one very special success story, Mrs. Florence McAvoy. She was a seventy-six year-old, bilateral, below-knee amputee with diabetes and glaucoma and probably other related illnesses. She was a beautiful Black woman with a gentle nature and a strong, determined spirit. Mrs. McAvoy was small framed with hazel eyes and soft, straight, silver hair that she wore pinned up. She reminded me of

Mama although Mama was younger. Apparently, her daughter made a promise to her that if she could walk, she could come home. A promise I'm sure she thought she would never have to honor. But Mrs. McAvoy was determined, and so was I.

When I initiated her treatment program, she had one healed stump and a recently amputated stump, which was not healing very well. In addition to range of motion and therapeutic exercises, we began daily whirlpools, debridement and dressing of the unhealed stump, followed by ambulatory activities with her prosthesis. As time went on, she got stronger, the stump healed, we got a new prosthesis, and Mrs. McAvoy was walking with a walker and bilateral prostheses. Although she couldn't walk marathons, she eventually got to the point where she could walk out of that nursing home into a taxi, sit down, cross her legs, and ride HOME. That was probably the longest and most frightening walk of her life, but she did it! The greatest thing I learned from working in the nursing homes was to LIVE YOUR LIFE now, while you have the ability, for truly, tomorrow is not promised. Everybody dies, but not everybody lives. Yesterday is history, tomorrow is a mystery, and all we have is the gift of today, which is why they call it the present.

In 1979, I became a consultant for John and Sam, two Jewish physical therapists, who had contracts with many facilities throughout Brooklyn. The late seventies had brought the growing popularity of consultants vs. full time employees with benefits. I began consulting for them during my second year as a licensed physical therapist. I was still living in the East Village, and the subway system was my sole means of transport. On average, I took about ten trains a day, travelling from facility to facility, passing my time on the trains by reading the N.Y. Times and trying to follow the stock market. Or, for motivation, I would count up my work hours for the week. I was being paid on a fee for service basis, so the more hours, the more money, which made for very long days. It didn't take long to realize that if I cut out the middle man and started establishing my own contracts, I would make even more money, so to John and Sam's shock and dismay, that's what I did. I was their only Black physical therapist, and many of their contracts were with predominantly Black owned facilities, so they were none too happy when I went independent, especially when we began competing for some of the same facilities. Being a direct provider, I could always under bid them. It seemed they considered me indentured to them, and they grew a bit hostile, but we didn't have a contract and anything advertised in the newspapers was fair game.

By 1980 I was making even more money, having established a few nursing home contracts of my own. I bought my first car that year, a red sports sedan with a stick shift and sunroof. She was pretty. I didn't have a driver's license yet and was ill prepared to drive a stick shift. To further demonstrate my ignorance of car ownership, I paid full sticker price in Manhattan. I drove my car home from the dealership at 6th Avenue, and 17th Street to 1st Avenue and 9th Street, jerking and stalling all the way home. Manhattan wasn't as crowded back then, and people were a bit more tolerant, so fortunately, we made it home without incident. I bought a bottle of wine and sat on my fourth floor walk-up windowsill. Looking down at my brand new, shiny, expensive automobile I thought, wow, you really did it. It was quite intimidating.

I managed to jerk and stall myself around town to my jobs and to the clubs. I even drove to the road tests that I would fail. I drove everywhere I wanted to go, until I didn't jerk and stall anymore. I even took a road trip with no driver's license to the Florida Cays with my brother, Cliff, and my girlfriend, Gia, and I was no longer intimidated. I did finally pass the road test on my third attempt. Cliff told me afterwards that every time my mother knew that I was about to drive somewhere, she would frantically call and tell him, "She's getting behind the wheel again!" Perhaps the fact that I would have some sort of collision about every three months didn't give her much confidence in my driving. It got to the point that I would just wait until all four sides of the car were dented before I would put it in the shop for repairs. Thanks to God (and it could only have been Him), I never hurt anyone or myself too seriously during my many, many auto accidents throughout the years.

My use of cocaine increased during the early eighties, mostly on the weekends when it was time to party. Conveniently, there were a lot of drugs to be had right down the street from where I lived. East of 1st Avenue were Avenues A, B, C & D consecutively, otherwise known as Alphabet City. This area of the East Village consisted mostly of abandoned buildings and shells of buildings inhabited by squatters and drug dealers. Before going to the club, I would pull up in front of one of these buildings in my new car, park illegally, and proceed inside to buy some coke for the evening. Now understand, with money in my pockets I was dressed to go out, looking good and smelling good. I would boldly walk into these abandoned buildings, sometimes having to navigate across beams because there was no floor, standing in line with junkies and other questionable characters to wait my turn at the hole in the door, where I would hand my money to another hand who in turn would hand back my drug order. Sometimes, if I was in a rush, I wouldn't even wait in line. I would just kind of demand permission to jump the line, and they always let me go ahead without any protests. Maybe they thought I was a cop or just out of my freaking mind.

First of all, I shouldn't have been parking right in front

of the buildings because they were always under police surveillance. Secondly, I was all dressed up and clearly had money, walking around in abandoned buildings with junkies and undesirables. Yet, never did I fall through a floor or get mugged, raped, or even busted by the police. They say God watches over children and fools, and I certainly wasn't a child anymore.

My brother, Clifford, was also becoming increasingly involved with cocaine use at the time, along with other felonious activities. He went home one day to inform my mother that the Mafia was after him, and she would have to uproot her life and leave her apartment and job on Staten Island to avoid being hurt or killed. My mother complied, and she and my sister temporarily moved in with me, in my tenement on East 9th Street until she got an apartment in the Bronx on Sedgewick Avenue. Her life would never be the same.

Mama and Papa were still on Staten Island at the time. Mama had already retired, so she could take care of Papa full time. She didn't drive, and after Mommy left Staten Island, Mama was there alone to care for herself and her husband. I was in a pretty stable relationship, still living on East 9th Street. My lover (that was the term for a same sex partner in those days), Gia, and I decided to live together. In my heart I knew I wasn't really ready for a lifelong commitment, but Gia, an attractive nurse, wanted to be a wife, and she was good at it. After subleasing my apartment on East 9th Street, we moved to Staten Island so I could be around to help Mama if she needed me.

Gia and I rented a luxury apartment on Victory Boulevard. We noticed how everyone had several locks on their doors, but it didn't register at the time, not until we were robbed the second month we were there. The first month, my car was stolen. I stayed home the day after the robbery, believing they would return for the new carpet that was rolled up in the living room awaiting installation. They did. I was lying in bed, smoking some herb and watching TV when I saw figures creeping across my terrace. No, it wasn't the herb. I called the police and ran out the front door, but then I realized I had left the herb on the dresser, so I went back in to put it away. As I proceeded to run back out the front door, the police were coming in the door. One cop kicked me dead in the chest, right in the solar plexus. I fell to the ground, the wind completely knocked out of me. He was reaching for his gun, but I couldn't speak. Tears began to roll out of my eyes as I gasped to try to utter a word.

He must have seen my desperation, "Do you live here?"

"Yes, yes," I finally blurted out.

He took his hand off his gun and instructed me that I must not leave my front door open after I've reported a break-in. When I tell this story to people most of them expect me to be outraged that he kicked me and didn't apologize. I was thankful that it was a clean kick straight to the solar plexus and that he didn't shoot me. Staten Island had a very racist overtone back then.

Gia and I broke up shortly afterwards. I went to live with my mother in the Bronx and Mama and Papa moved to Coop City in the same complex where my aunts resided. Thus, our exodus from Staten Island. You can't go home again.

Mommy's apartment in the Bronx was unique and very cool. After living with her for a couple of months, she arranged for me to get the apartment right next door to hers. It was fabulous; it had two bedrooms, one and a half bathrooms, and an enclosed terrace with views of the Harlem River and Manhattan. So, here we are in the Bronx, back together again. Neither of us was prepared for what the next few years were to bring.

THE BEASTS

The unsaids and unremembereds began to surface almost immediately after my mother's death. They would impose themselves upon me early in the morning as I was preparing to go to work. One moment I'd be in the shower washing, singing to music; the next moment, I'm crumbled on the shower floor sobbing, bathed in shame and anger. "*Why didn't she protect me?*" I'd scream in my head. I wouldn't have allowed my child to see me beaten over and over and over again. And after the beatings were done, it still wasn't over because the black eyes and busted lips and swollen face took weeks to heal. So every time I looked at my mother, it was like reliving it again and again. The abused spouse is not the only victim of domestic violence, the children suffer equally, if not more.

"Why didn't she love *me* enough to leave?" would echo in my mind and break my heart. And I would sob for little Mellie, all alone and unprotected, trying to be brave and be the protector. Trying to be self-sufficient, so I wouldn't have to bother anyone. I would sob and sob, and then I'd just get inconsolably angry. It's almost impossible to mourn someone with whom you are angry. I think by then, I was mourning more for myself and for my lost youth, rather than for my mother.

Deeply buried memories of the molestation began to

surface. Didn't I behave differently afterwards, I wondered? Could no one see? Was I so insignificant that no one even bothered to notice? The questions haunted me. The vision of my so-called grandfather—my biological father's stepfather, Mr. Thompson—laying me down on their living room couch, pulling down my little panties and licking in between my legs, telling me he wanted to make me feel good and how it was our secret. Visions of lying in bed with my grandmother, Agatha, my father's mother, pretending to be asleep, while she allowed me to play with her breasts—haunting visions. What a freak show those two had going on with little four-year-old me right in the middle. *"If they weren't dead, I'd kill them!"* This I would shout in the shower after my sob fest, wanting only to wash down the drain with the dirty, used water. But I had to get to work. After all, there was money to be made and patients to be healed.

Somehow, I would manage to pull myself together, put on my game face, get dressed, and spray on some perfume. It was the mid-eighties, a time of big hair, shoulder pads, and lots of perfume. Clinique was my favorite fragrance at the time. I would get into my car and drive from the Bronx to Brooklyn, a little over an hour's drive, traffic permitting. I was employed at Nostrand Medical Center, which was part of an HMO. I was director of physical therapy with a staff of one—*me*. It was ideal, and I loved it there. I had worked diligently and faithfully for many years to obtain that position. My career was my saving grace during Mommy's illness and subsequent death. It was my lifeline, my escape, and my purpose for existence.

Around the time of Mommy's death, the Oprah Winfrey show premiered. I think it was the first time that people were able to publicly reveal some of their most sensitive issues. It must have been a season of revelation and the seeking of resolution. There truly are seasons and times for everything.

The Bible states in Ecclesiastes 3:1, "There is a time for everything, and a season for every activity under heaven." Check it out if you are unfamiliar with this scripture. Anyway, that was back in the days of the video cassette recorder. I used to watch soap operas back then, a pastime that started in college. In fact, the first soap opera I watched was with my grandmother, Agatha, my father's mother. I recall going to visit her one day during my junior college years. Her husband had long since passed away. She didn't have much to say. She just stared at the TV screen watching, "As the World Turns." She probably couldn't bear to look at me, guilt-ridden as she should have been. I just looked on kind of oblivious, having suppressed all memories of her and her husband's evil doings.

After my mother's death, the bright spot of my day became rushing home to see the day's recordings on the VCR: "All My Children," "One Life to Live," and "General Hospital," followed by Oprah. On the way home from work, I would pick up something for dinner, usually a steak or something quick, but first I would stop in Washington Heights for some coke, the drug, that is. Fortunately for me, during the years of my cocaine use, I never really had a good connection for quality cocaine. Had I, who knows where I'd be now. So, I would spend my evenings sniffing coke, drinking cognac, smoking cigarettes, and watching soap operas, attempting to allay my pain after spending the day trying to remediate the pain of others.

That year, the year Mommy died, the year of the VCR and soap operas, cognac, and cocaine, was the year I began to discover that I had issues, the year I began to find myself, if only in realizing that I was losing myself. That, in fact, I had lost myself long ago. That year began my downward spiral into loss after loss after loss, until I had nothing left to lose but my health and what was left of my mind. That "year" went on for over seven years—work, soap operas, cognac, cigarettes, and the losses. I was drowning in the smoke and ashes.

Papa was the first to pass away, a year after Mommy's death. He was my grandfather, Mama's husband, who had Alzheimer's for many years and who shared the bed with my mother as she lay there dying, as they both lay there dying. Papa was completely mentally incapacitated and helpless, and Mama took care of them both. She changed their diapers, fed them, and cleaned them. I never thought about all Mama was doing until now. Wow. I was present again, there in Mama's bedroom when Papa died. My aunts (my mother's sisters) and some of my cousins were there also. We were all having drinks and chatting, just hanging out as we so often did, when Mama discovered that Papa had stopped breathing. My cousin and I, both health care professionals, began to administer CPR, but to no avail. There was no EMS called this time.

There was a death every year after Mommy died, friends and family. In 1989, my mother's older sister, Barbara, passed from heart disease. We had almost lost her a couple of years earlier, but God blessed her with extra time, unfinished business I suppose. During that time, I think she tried to convey to us the importance of living your life fully. I remember her telling me one day, "Sometimes I'm invited places, and I don't really feel up to going, but then I make the effort, and I'm always glad I went."

Aunt Barbara was the intellectual of the family. She valued intellect and education as much as Mommy valued beauty and femininity. When I was about four or five, at every family gathering, Aunt Barbara would pull out the N.Y. Times and demand everyone's attention. "Watch this, watch this; go ahead Melanie, read." I would then read the lead story of the day as Aunt Barbara proudly stood by my side. Soon it was established throughout the family that I was highly intelligent, and I had potential for greatness.

Aunt Barbara gave this to me, this sense of worth, of value. I grew up believing that I was smart and that I was special. That belief gave me the confidence to be competitive in school and helped me to be successful in life. I'm so sorry that I didn't have then the appreciation that I have now, and that I didn't even realize how she changed my life. How she saved my life. She gave me that one glimmer of hope and self-esteem in an otherwise hopeless, hapless childhood. One never knows, how life-changing an encouraging word can be.

Words have such great power. They can be blessings or curses. The Bible tells us that "the power of life and death is in the tongue," and so it is. Please, be mindful what you say to your children. Your words can make or break them, so be very careful. It's sad how when we are younger, we rarely appreciate our family, our friends, our lives. We take for granted that they will always be there, and we will always be here. What do they say? "If I knew then what I know now."

It was around 1989, when I realized I had to stop doing cocaine. I couldn't breathe. My nasal passage was extremely inflamed from all the garbage I had snorted up my nose. It was enough already. I knew I couldn't do it alone, and I wasn't going back into rehab, so I started going to church instead.

Growing up, we attended a Catholic Church, St. Mary's. On occasion, Mommy would send my brother, sister, and me to church with a quarter for collection. We would stop at Caroline's penny candy store and get a brown paper bag full of candy with a dime left over for collection. Back then the service was in Latin, so basically, we just sat there for an hour watching the pomp and circumstance while eating our candy. What else was there to do?

I hadn't really attended church since I was a child. Occasionally, I would seek out a church as I always had the need to be... what? Good? A Christian? Maybe just good enough? I don't know how I defined it in my mind back then, but there was always a draw, a lingering, sometimes elusive knowledge that God and the Bible were the answer. Perhaps I felt this way because I had praying grandparents, Mama and Papa, that is. Anyway, I started attending St. Nicholas of Tolentine, a local Catholic church. Whenever I entered any church, I always felt *less than*, like everyone in the church was so "holy" and I was so lowly, this big unworthy sinner— the smoking, drinking, cursing, drug taking homosexual. How ungodly was I! By 1989, the Catholic Church had changed. The service was in English. St. Nicholas is a beautiful gothic style church with a bell tower, stained glass windows, statues, crucifixes and all. It is on Fordham Road in the Bronx, which begins the boundary of what is called the South Bronx. The congregation, then, was mostly middle to lower class Hispanics, with some Blacks and Whites intermingled throughout.

The service itself did not make that much of an impact on me. I didn't feel part of the church or the congregation. I just needed to be closer to God, nearer to His presence, so He could hear me and help me. "Come near to me and I will come near to you," He tells us. I needed to be near Him. I wasn't a Christian, per se, but I knew my salvation depended upon being close to Him. I went to church feeling "less than" the rest of the congregation, but I went anyway because I needed to.

I don't recall any condemning sermons at St. Nicholas of Tolentine. In fact, the priests strived to be very inclusive. They even wore kente cloth during Kwanza. So where did all these sinful feelings, these feelings of guilt and condemnation come from? We are exposed to so many opinions and

The Beasts

prejudices throughout our lives, so many condemnations directly or indirectly. We are always never good enough for some people, always somehow inadequate in something, no? We all hurt and have our insecurities.

I continued to go to church. I also prayed every day. I read the Bible and prayed some more. And you know what? I haven't used cocaine since. God did free me! I didn't go to St. Nicholas of Tolentine for long, maybe for a few months, but it was long enough for me to draw near to Him and Him to me. I could breathe freely again at least as freely as my cigarettes would allow. I stopped doing coke, but I hadn't entered sainthood yet.

After Aunt Barbara's demise, the deaths persisted year after year, loss after loss. I continued to go to work and make a lot of money and come home and drink, smoke, and watch my VCR, entertaining my pain. At least by this time I was finally beginning to realize just how much pain I had. It seemed that all the pain I had denied almost all my life began to make a gaping hole in the center of my soul and was slowly but quite surely sucking me in, devouring me.

I had a girlfriend, Dana, with whom I managed to maintain a dysfunctional relationship. We were both quite emotionally challenged at the time with our own separate issues. When we were together, we were extremely passionate. Our passion was expressed either sexually or physically (fighting). It was quite a consuming relationship. After six years, neither of us could take it anymore, so we parted before we killed each other. All the while, my pain manifested itself more and more, like some morose beast that had escaped captivity, never to be reigned in again. The beast was free and quite visible for all to see. I gradually but surely became quite a downer to my family, my friends, and even myself.

While I spent weekdays with my patients and "all my children, et al," drinking and pacifying the beast, I spent my weekends partying and looking for love. Most Saturday nights I would find myself driving with one eye closed so I wouldn't see double as I careened down the highway to home. Again, thanks only to God, I never seriously hurt myself or anyone else during my drunken escapades about town.

One evening, when it was still light, I was driving home from my cousin's house. Having consumed only a few glasses of wine, I felt perfectly fine. She lived across town, twenty minutes from my home. I was on Gun Hill Road and didn't think I was speeding. All of a sudden, my car hit the curb on my side of the road, which sent it into a ninety degree turn, uncontrollably crossing the lane of oncoming traffic. Passing a group of guys playing dominoes, I crashed into a fire hydrant on the opposite sidewalk and ended up in the side of a building. I probably would have been dead if the fire hydrant, which peeled off the whole driver's side of my car, didn't slow my roll. The guys came running over to my aid, insisting I get out of the car because they assumed I had been drinking. I told them to mind their business and tried to start the car so I could leave the scene before the police arrived. Not drunk, eh?

The police arrived, called a tow truck, and asked me if I needed to go to the hospital. I declined and instead waited in my car for the tow truck while the police waited in their car. I wanted to light a cigarette, but alas, the cigarette lighter in my car didn't work, so I took my intoxicated self over to the cops to ask them for a light. When the first cop told me he didn't have a match (with apparent attitude), I returned the attitude and said, "I wasn't talking to you. I was talking to the nice officer over there." Why they didn't give me a sobriety test or just lock my drunk butt up, I'll never know. Actually, I do know, the Grace of God, My Father. I'm just so very thankful I didn't kill or injure anyone that night. Five feet to the left, and I would have mowed down those domino players. Thank You, Lord!

My family has always been pretty close knit, especially my immediate family, Mama and Papa's children and their children. We would often gather for family reunions, parties, and what became all too often, funerals. After a few drinks, the beast would feel free to rear its ugly head. I felt the need to start divulging the fact that I was molested when I was a child. No one really wanted to hear it. I was just looking for an explanation or maybe vindication. How could anyone not know? I know I told my grandmother, Agatha, the molester herself and the wife of the other molester. She was bathing me one day and washed in between my legs. I remember saying to her, "Grandpa does that." She just looked at me scornfully and said, "Don't lie on Grandpa." I told her I wasn't lying, but she angrily said, "Don't ever say that again," and I guess I didn't. She must have been his co-conspirator, otherwise how did I end up alone in the house with him long enough for him to molest me, especially since he slept in the basement? If Grandma didn't even allow him to sleep on the same floor as she, much less the same room, why is she leaving me alone with him? But like I said, I forgive them, sick as they were, and I have healed. Glory to God.

Anyway, one evening at a family gathering, my cousin Ralph and I were talking. He has always been very astute and perceptive. As children, we spent a lot of time together at Mama and Papa's apartment on Staten Island. He was like an older brother in some ways. During our conversation that evening, out of the clear blue, he said, "You used to be such a happy child, always playful and then one day you just changed. You became withdrawn for some reason." I could have cried. I could have kissed him, but all I could say was, "I was molested." My God, finally the vindication. I WAS DIFFERENT! IT WAS VISIBLE! He just said, "Hmnn, I knew it was something." Ralph helped me to heal that night. He helped me to begin to slay the beast.

During my time here on earth, I've heard many, *too* many horrifying stories of child abuse. We've all heard of or known someone or maybe even personally experienced unspeakable acts of abuse as children. As a middle class American citizen, it is hard for me to fathom children being sold as sex slaves or being amputated or blinded sometimes by their own parents to become more productive street beggars, but the reality is, it happens to hundreds, maybe thousands of children every day.

Even in America, land of the free and home of the brave, the incidence of molestation and abuse of children is extreme. The publication, Preventing Child Maltreatment, volume 19, number 2, 2009 states, "Sizable portions of U.S. adults report a history of sexual abuse--thirty to forty percent of women and thirteen percent of men in one analysis." I wonder how many incidents go unreported? How many of us out there are just walking wounded? The children are not free, and the abusers are far from brave.

The publication further cites, "Offenders are overwhelmingly male, ranging from adolescents to the elderly." And by the way, not predominantly homosexual men, as some would have you believe.

And the victims? The American Psychological Association as well as many other authorities on the subject agree that children and adolescents who have been sexually abused can suffer a range of psychological and behavioral problems from mild to severe, in both the short and long term. These problems typically include depression, anxiety, guilt, fear, sexual dysfunction, withdrawal and acting out. The negative effects of child sexual abuse can affect the victim for many years and into adulthood. Adults who were sexually abused as children commonly experience depression. Additionally, high levels of anxiety in these adults can result in self-destructive behavior, such as alcoholism or drug abuse, anxiety attacks, situation specific anxiety disorders, and insomnia. Many victims also encounter problems in their adult relationships and in their adult sexual functioning. [I can hear the self-righteous homophobes, right about now, "You see, that's why she's a lesbian." Not quite that simple, people.] Revictimization is also a common phenomenon in people abused as children. In short, the ill effects of child sexual abuse are wide ranging. There is no one set of symptoms or outcomes that victims experience.

I am so thankful to God (and Hollis) that compared to what so many others have experienced, my childhood sexual trauma seems minimal. Yet it still had a devastating effect on me for quite a long period of my life. I knew I had completely recovered, when in writing this book, I decided to give details and not just refer to the molestation as I had done in the past. And when I recalled and recorded the details, my face did not become flushed with shame as had invariably happened in the past. Although I initially felt anger while in total recall, I did not remain angry. I have peace about what happened to me, knowing that God is my true vindicator. As He says, "Vengeance is mine." Well, I leave Mr. and Mrs. Thompson to Him.

Healing doesn't come without work and faith. Paula White, minister and author, states, "You can't conquer what you don't confront, and you can't confront what you don't identify." The American Psychological Association has concluded, children who are able to confide in a trusted adult and who are believed, experience less trauma than children who do not disclose the abuse.

Joyce Meyer is another minister on Christian television whose teachings have been instrumental in my healing process. She keeps it real and clear. She was subject to sexual abuse for many years of her childhood at the hands of her father. Her ministry is called "Enjoying Everyday Life," and now, glory to God, that is just what she does. In one of her books, *Beauty for Ashes*, she shares how she overcame her pain through the love of God. The term, "beauty for ashes" comes from the Bible, Is. 61:1-3 which states, "The Spirit of the sovereign Lord is on me... to proclaim the year of the Lord's favor and the day of vengeance of our God, to comfort all who mourn, ...Instead of their shame my people will receive a double portion, and instead of disgrace they will rejoice...everlasting joy will be theirs."

I'm here to tell you, God does keep His promise. If we open our hearts to Him, He will heal them.

As for those of you who hurt children, well they say, "hurting people, hurt people." GET HELP! Personally, I think the worst thing anyone can do is hurt a child in any way. So GET HEALED! May God help you! And in the words of Forrest Gump, "That's all I have to say about that."

THE GREATEST LOSSES

Mama died in 1992. She had worked hard all her life until she retired to take care of her husband, who had prematurely become unable to take care of himself. Prior to her death, she had been living with my Aunt Joan, her youngest and only surviving daughter. Mama had a brain tumor or something like that. I stopped paying attention to the details of my friends' and family's terminalities a few deaths after my mother's. I just couldn't stand to think of the details anymore nor cope with the futility of the whole situation.

Mama and I always remained close. I like to think I was her favorite grandchild. One day, Aunt Joan informed everyone it was time to come up to her house and say goodbye to Mama. She was on hospice care, receiving daily pain control treatment from a visiting nurse. The nurse seemed to know the exact day that Mama would pass, so we all went up the day before to say good-bye. It was just like all the rest of our family gatherings, drinking, smoking, laughing, crying.

Mama was lying in my aunt's bed. We each went in individually to say our good-byes. As I reflect on the whole scene, I wonder what Mama must have thought, each one coming in with alcohol and cigarette smoke on their breath; while the others were in the living room, drinking, chatting, and laughing. In retrospect, it seems almost disrespectful to me now. Perhaps it was actually reassuring to Mama. Life would go on. We would all be there for each other, drinking, smoking, laughing, and crying. Come to think about it, it was almost like a testimonial. Mama was the one who always kept us all together, in communication with one another or about one another. And she was always right there along with us drinking, smoking, laughing, crying, until she got ill. She was a strong, brave, kind, loving, loyal, insightful, hardworking woman. She was my Mama.

Mama and me

There is a gospel song by Helen Baylor called "Praying Grandmother." In it she speaks about her life, how she got involved with drugs and almost died. She says, "The devil was trying to kill me, but I had a praying grandmother." My Mama was a "praying grandmother" 'cause surely the devil had been trying to kill me. I don't remember what I said to Mama before she died. I hope I thanked her for all she had done for me and for all of us. I know I told her I loved her. And this time, I did get the opportunity to kiss my grandmother good-bye.

When my brother Cliff arrived at Mama's wake, he didn't look very well. He sat in a corner most of the evening. That night, the night before the funeral, Cliff; my sister, Carla; and my good friend Vincent (who had AIDS) spent the night at my apartment in the Bronx. I stayed with my then current partner Maria. Mama was buried the next day alongside Mommy and Papa. Cliff came home with me to spend the night after the funeral.

Even though our relationship had some trying moments, Cliff and I were best of friends. We used to party together occasionally. Cliff was also gay. In fact, for a couple of years before Mommy died, Cliff and his partner Juan, Mommy, and I all lived next door to one another, Cliff and Juan on one side, me on the other, and Mommy in the middle. I wonder how she reacted to Cliff when she found out that he was gay. I don't think I ever discussed it with either one of them. For sure it was probably not as vitriolic as her reaction to my coming out. I paved the way for the rest of my gay family members. I have a few gay cousins, whose coming out was received with a bit more acceptance. Mommy delighted in having her two gay children around. She would cook, and we would all hang out, have drinks, laugh and enjoy each other's company. On Friday nights Cliff, Juan, my girlfriend, and I would jump in my car with a bottle of wine and some herb and go to the Whitestone drive-in theater to see horror movies. These were some of the best times of my life.

During my cocaine days, we often got high together. Unfortunately for Cliff, in the late eighties he became deeply involved with the whole drug and party scene, especially after Mommy died. He was smart and very handsome, but like all of us, Cliff had issues. Drugs brought him low for a while, but he was able to pull himself out of it somehow, with no rehab program and no therapy. I'm not quite sure how he did it; it could only have been the grace of God. We had to part ways for a while when things got really bad. But I always loved him; he was my best friend.

By the early 1990s, he had completely cleaned up. He travelled around Europe and North Africa for a time with one of his wealthy friends. He even started working at Harlem Hospital. He was back to his charming, sensitive, witty, handsome self. Cliff got an apartment on 183rd Street in Manhattan, not far from me, a fourth floor walk-up. We would meet on weekends and play tennis or walk across the George Washington Bridge and go for Indian food afterwards. He would come over to my apartment and if music was playing sometimes we would dance and goof around. He would pick me up, spin me around, much to my protest, and then we would just laugh. He was quite strong for his size. We hung out together a lot. He even wrote me a poem once, telling me how much he loved me and how good I had been to him and my family. I loved him so much. We relied on and confided in one another.

So, the night of Mama's funeral, Cliff came home with me. My sister, Carla; her husband; and daughter also must have spent the night before they left in the morning for Ohio. That's where my sister chose to flee to lick her wounds after Mommy's death, Ohio. I went to work the following day because that's what I did; I worked. That's what kept me busy and sane and away from the pain for a little while. When I returned from work that evening, Cliff was on the couch in the same place I left him that morning.

"Hey, what's wrong with you, Cliff? You haven't gotten up all day?"

He hardly moved, "No, I don't feel well. Got any juice?'

"If you want some juice, you need to get up and get it

yourself." Then I looked at him closely, and all I could feel was fear. His eyes seemed half dazed, and his skin was ashen. All during Mama's funeral proceedings and the activity afterwards, I didn't notice just how ill my brother was. He held it together until we got home; then, I guess he just had to give in to it. All I wanted at that moment was for him to get up and be well. But he couldn't.

I got the juice for him and told him, "If you really can't get up, I'm gonna have to call 911." I suppose I thought I would coax him/frighten him into being well.

But he just shut his eyes and moaned, "Call them."

As soon as the paramedics arrived, they knew his diagnosis because his throat was covered with thrush. Thrush is a white yeast infection in the mouth and throat, usually found in people with AIDS. My brother had AIDS! And he never even told me. So, one night after burying Mama, I am in the emergency room with my brother, my best friend, who now has full blown AIDS.

Immediately after Cliff was released from the hospital, I got him an apartment in my building. As president of the co-op board, I was able to get a month to month lease for him, for which I paid the rent. He could no longer maneuver the four flights of stairs at his apartment, and I didn't want him to be a shut-in. He had a home health aide to help him with all his ADL's (activities of daily living). The second day he was home, he came down to my apartment in a wheelchair, his home health aide pushing him.

"Look at me," he said in a gruff, pitiful voice. I could hardly do it. I continued to go to work, heal my patients, come home, drink, smoke and watch soap operas. I would visit Cliff first, but I could hardly stand it. My brother was dying. He was bitter. I was hurt and angry and frightened. He was probably all of those things, too. Why was he dying so soon? Lots of people lived for a long time with AIDS. His ex, Juan, had AIDS before Cliff was diagnosed, and he was still alive in 2009 when I began this book. Why didn't he tell me? He had to know. Perhaps that's why he straightened up and got a job, so he could have health insurance.

We never had that discussion. We did have the opportunity to go away together during his illness. I took him to Grand Cayman, one of my favorite places, to my friend's house on the beach. He was weak and frail, but we managed to do a few things on the island. We even went on a very short boat ride. I am thankful we were able to have some quality time together, and wish I remembered more of it. When we returned home, Cliff spent the remainder of his days in great discomfort, in and out of the hospital. I remember sitting on the couch with him one day, holding his hand. I burst into tears. "I love you, but I want this to be over." I didn't mean I wanted him dead, but I couldn't stand to see him suffer anymore. He looked like Mommy just before she died. His beautiful face, thin and sunken, was barely able to contain his big, radiant, once piercing, now, frightened eyes. His head, bald, like Mommy's after her cancer treatments. They both even wore blue robes during their last days. I tenderly held his bony, ashen hand in mine, and we just cried.

Shortly afterwards, Cliff was hospitalized again. Maria, my partner, decided that I needed to get away for a weekend, so she made reservations for us at a bed and breakfast in Cape May, New Jersey. The grief and stress was beginning to permeate my soul and engulf my demeanor. Before we left town, I went to visit Cliff in the hospital. The hospital staff had been trying to get me to sign a DNR (do not resuscitate) order, but I just couldn't, so each time I visited, I avoided it and them. When I arrived at Cliff's room, he was tied to a chair with sheets. I told him I was going away for the weekend and that our cousin was going to check in on him. He asked me to untie him, which I did attempt to do, but the

Me and Cliff

the early years

the good years

Me and Cliff

the last year

the last days

knots were too tight. Cliff had become very difficult during his illness, very angry and uncooperative at times.

I surmised they must have tied him in a sitting position to help him avoid getting pneumonia from lying down too much, so I decided to leave him as he was and explained to him why. I kissed him good-bye and told him I loved him and would see him on Monday. He told me he loved me, too. My cousin called later that evening. Cliff was gone.

I wish I had untied him.

Just like Mommy, who died six months after she was diagnosed, Cliff died six months after he was diagnosed, six months after we buried Mama—six long/short months. I miss him most of all.

By this time, 1992, I had given up all my contracts in the nursing homes and was focused totally on my private practice/employment at the HMO, whose building they had recently remodeled. It became my responsibility to design, plan, administrate, and operate a brand new, state of the art physical therapy department. It was comprised of a small suite of rooms with its own reception area. This was my baby, and I attended to every detail and every aspect of getting her up and running. In very little time, I had established a thriving practice. It was absolutely perfect. The HMO employed me full time to treat their patients; they provided health and retirement benefits and they allowed me to treat my private patients. They even matched my 401K contributions, to which I contributed practically my whole check. It was peanuts compared to what I was making from my private practice. Eventually, when things got so busy and I needed some help, they provided a receptionist for me, so I no longer had to employ my own administrative assistant. I loved my practice. I loved my patients. This was good. *This* was what I had worked so hard for, diligently, desperately through the pain.

The HMO was a physician-owned practice. My success became quite apparent to the physicians when I pulled up on Eastern Parkway in my brand new luxury car. I was making so much money that when the HMO informed me that they could no longer match my 401K contribution, it didn't matter. I was hot! I looked good, smelled good and no longer spent my evenings with the usual cast of characters. I was still drinking, but not alone; Maria and I drank together, with Pinot Grigio wine replacing the cognac. The pain seemed as though it was beginning to subside.

One afternoon in 1994, the chief physician of the group called me into his office to inform me that they had decided to contract out the physical therapy services so they could use my suite for doctors' offices. I was devastated. It was as if someone kicked me in the chest and knocked all the wind out of me. This was the catalyst that catapulted me to the edge of the darkness. I couldn't believe what I was hearing. I had worked so hard, had given this job my best for almost fifteen years. This was my home, my refuge, my greatest accomplishment, and now this, too, was being taken away from me. What the hell!

I didn't go quietly into the night this time. I couldn't start a petition to stop my mother from being taken away, or Mama, or Papa, or Cliff, or Aunt Barbara, or Vincent, or my cousin, or other friends I had lost to AIDS. No petition would have kept them from being stolen from me, all taken before their time, all within the previous nine years, one a year, two in '92. No petitions for them, just good-byes.

But this I could fight. My patients all loved me and were disturbed by the loss of their physical therapist, but our petitions had no effect. It was a done deal. During my last days at the HMO, I tried to remain strong and focused. I looked into leasing an office in the area and opening my own clinic, but that would have been like starting all over again. I was angry. I didn't come this far to start over and going backwards was not an option. I was not going to start running from nursing home to nursing home again as someone's employee, making a fraction of my current income. I was just so damn tired of losing everyone and everything I cared about. I couldn't take one bit more. No, no more. I give up!

Losing my practice became the most critical loss of all. It was the one constant in my life, my refuge, where I had some control. My life as I had known it, had come to a complete halt. For the past twenty years, I had focused on my professional career. It was who I was. I was making more money than just about anyone in my family had ever made. Respected, needed, and valued, I was good at what I did and loved doing it. Helping others to heal was my calling and my joy. What I hadn't realized was that I was in dire need of healing, myself. But God knew it! All I knew was that now I

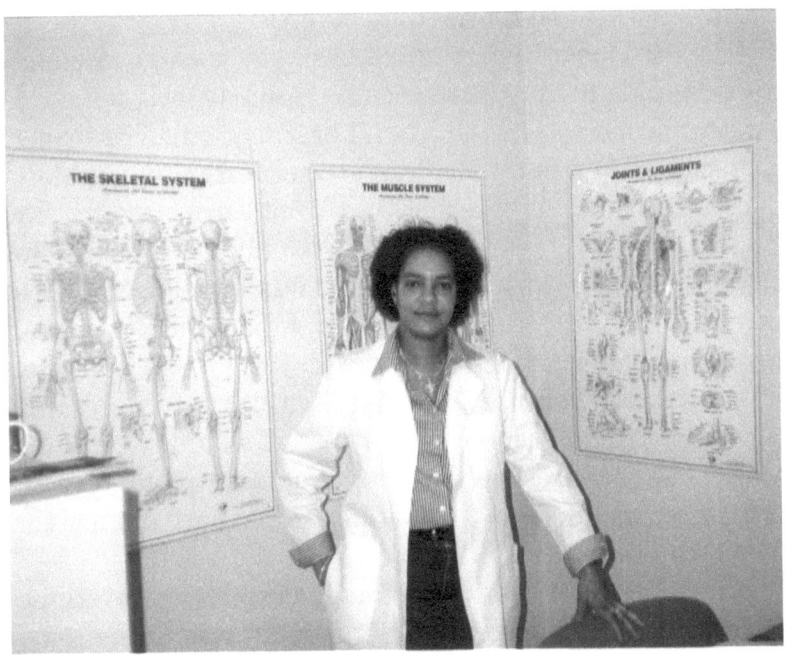

was completely lost. My identity, Melanie E. Lewis, Physical Therapist, was gone. "Oh, God, what now?" I thought. "It's all over."

But it was a set-up. For instance, just a few months prior to losing my practice, my cousin solicited me to buy disability insurance. I took out a policy with him. Around the same time another company solicited me, and I got a policy with them also. Fortunately or unfortunately, as the case may be, my occupation and numerous car accidents, compounded with a recent injury sustained at a private patient's home had all taken its toll on my body, leaving me with subsequent cervical and lumbar spinal complications. In other words, neck and back injuries. It was time to succumb to the pain—physical, mental, and emotional, time to surrender to ALL of it. So I did, and collected disability insurance in the interim. Combined, I was receiving about two-thirds of my income, approximately twelve thousand dollars a month. I could live with that for the time being.

I couldn't bear to stay home everyday with my feelings, my thoughts, and my memories, so I joined Maria at her real estate office. It was kind of cool. I had my own office again. I took classes and became a licensed real estate agent. Maria and I worked well together. We would drive around the Bronx looking for apartments to list or buildings to sell. But selling real estate was not my forte. I wasn't created for it. No matter how hard I tried, nothing ever materialized from all my efforts. When something is for you, it's for you, and when it's not, it's not. I didn't really care. Going to the office was just something to do, somewhere to be, so I wouldn't be home, alone. The days passed, one pretty much like another—go to the office, spend some time, come home, have dinner, and drink some wine.

But something was happening, despite my continual endeavors to just keep my life moving. I was losing touch with even the simplest of realities. Within six months of losing my practice, six months of collecting disability, the true enormity of my *disability* became painfully evident as it insidiously transformed to inability. The day I walked out of my apartment onto Fordham Road and everyone looked like some animated cartoon character, I knew something was undeniably and seriously wrong. My world had become surreal. I was untethered and set adrift. It was time to go.

The song by War, "Slipping Into Darkness," often ran through my mind, and I would sing it, slowly recognizing that it was exactly what was happening to me. Later in my spiritual walk, I learned it was all part of the process; it was time for me to face my demons. I didn't know where I was going physically or spiritually, but I knew I had to get away from where I was. I had to be alone. And at that time, I felt like I wanted to be alone forever. Didn't need a vacation; I needed isolation.

I began looking at homes for sale in the N.Y. Times, homes in the country. Maria and I went to look at one we had found in the newspaper. Though it wasn't suitable, we decided to visit the town nearby. It was quaint, and I remember a good friend once speaking very highly of the area. So we engaged a real estate broker to show us some available properties. His name was Paul. Sitting in the backseat of his car, my head resting on the window, I instructed him to show me the most remote properties he had, preferably somewhere on a mountaintop, far away from everyone. I was spent, mentally, physically, emotionally, and spiritually. I just wanted to settle in somewhere for the duration and ride this out, whatever it was, before I totally lost my mind. Just needed to go hide somewhere and lick my wounds.

All during this period of the deaths and the losses, I prayed regularly and read the Bible occasionally. I don't remember what I prayed for specifically, except when I prayed to be freed of the cocaine, and God answered my prayer. I must have petitioned God to spare me the loss of my mother, or my brother, or even my practice. But I guess He was not responding to petitions at that time, at least not the way I would have wanted Him to respond.

Anyway, after a few weekend visits to Upstate New York, Paul finally showed me my new home. It was not what I thought I was looking for, but I knew it was home. It wasn't on an isolated mountaintop, thank God, because the winters are pretty severe, and I would have experienced isolation on a level that I, even at my darkest moments, could not have handled. It was in a neighborhood, but with three and one-half acres, it offered enough land and privacy that if I chose not to, I did not have to see another human being. The house itself was frame with a lot of wood floors and features that gave it a warm feeling, and it had an abundance of windows to let in the light and to see the wildlife outdoors.

The property had a tennis court (wish Cliff was here now) and plenty of room for a pool (something I always longed for in the city). But what really sold me was an antiquated wooden swing set. I could see children, lots of children, playing here. This was home.

Although I purchased the house, I did not move upstate right away. The master bedroom required major renovation, and I didn't want to be there for all the commotion. In addition, I needed to sell my co-op apartment in the Bronx. For some reason I desperately needed to get rid of that apartment, beautiful as it was. The compulsion to sell it was inexplicable and somewhat irrational, but it had to go. The maintenance charges were relatively low, and I had a parking spot in the garage, so the logical thing would have been to keep it, sublease it, and let it appreciate in value. I was already a landlord by then, so this could have been just another rental unit. But something in me needed to be done with the whole thing. I knew I had to sell the apartment, resign as president of the co-op board, and just get off of Sedgewick Avenue. I had lived there for about twelve years. There had been many good times, but things had slowly spiraled downward, beyond my tolerance to bear.

In the beginning, after Mommy left her job on Staten Island and moved to the Bronx, she couldn't find a full-time job. Cliff wasn't working at all; Juan supported him for the most part. I was working over-time at the various nursing homes and at the HMO. Mommy even worked with me part-time as my physical therapy aide at one of the nursing homes. This was around 1982, when we were all living next door to each other. My sister had married a man of questionable character, joined the Air Force, and was stationed in the Philippines. She had a baby girl, Candice. My sister convinced my mother to care for her baby while she finished her military obligations.

Carla brought this screaming infant home to Mommy and returned to her base halfway around the globe. I could hear the baby crying day and night through my bedroom window. How could Mommy stand it? We tried swings and toys, whatever would provide some hope of allaying Candice's seemingly incessant cries for attention, but nothing worked for too long. How Mommy dealt with it, I'll never know. The only break my mother got was when she went to work part-time and left Candice with a babysitter in the building.

It seemed my brother and sister were always dumping some problem in my mother's lap which subsequently, somehow ended up in mine. In all fairness, there was a time when I was no walk in the park, either. In retrospect, I think we all shared some responsibility in Mommy's premature demise. Hollis, Clifford, Carla, Candice, the tobacco companies, Mommy herself, and I were all contributory elements.

My mother never got a reprieve. She went from one stressful drama to the next. Did she ever have a joyful moment, a peaceful moment?

My sister was soon discharged from the military and returned to the Bronx, where she lived with my mother, both of them unemployed. By this time Cliff and Juan had lost their apartment, so Cliff would visit my mother often. The responsibility fell on me to supplement the household, which after a while, I began to resent. I remember staying home from work one day. I got some coke (cocaine that is) and some cognac, got high, and watched TV. I just felt like, "screw it." If no one is going to work, why should I? So, I rebelled for the day, realizing I was getting sick of the responsibility of a family.

I was so against being tied down that I didn't even have living room furniture. I reluctantly bought a bedroom set when I first moved in, but in my living room I had a used Sony Trinitron TV, a beach chair, a stereo set, and my albums, which were all that I needed. Now, I had the responsibility of my entire family. Yeah, I resented it.

Inevitably, my mother got evicted from her apartment. I don't remember if I knew it was happening or if I didn't want to know. I do remember rushing down to housing court with the back rent. However, too late, the judge would not accept it. So, Mommy lost her apartment and everyone moved in with me. Again.

I had been subleasing my apartment on East 9th Street, but eventually I vacated it, and Mommy, Carla, and Candice moved there. My mother got a full-time job in a halfway house for troubled teens. She seemed to enjoy it very much. She loved living in Manhattan, even in my tub-in-the-kitchen tenement, fourth floor walk-up apartment. It seemed for the first time in a long time, she had some joy, some peace in her life, in the very apartment that twelve years earlier, she begged me not to rent. How ironic is that? That year, June 15, 1984, she turned fifty. I gave her a birthday party for which she was very grateful.

    No, I needed to get rid of this apartment. The Bronx apartment, that is. The walls had too many stories to tell. The shower had washed away too many of my tears. The floors could no longer bear the weight of my sorrow. It was time to go, there was nothing for me here any longer. I sold the apartment, at a loss. I didn't really care; I just wanted out. In 1995 I moved to my new home in Upstate New York.

MOTHERHOOD AND RECONCILIATION

I spent the first few years in my new upstate home acclimating to country living. There was much work required in taking care of a house and the grounds. I watched the gardener mow until I learned how to drive a tractor. (Tractor sounds more farmer-like than seated lawnmower.) I mowed the lawn, pruned the bushes, and even cut down trees with a chainsaw. Eventually, I managed the maintenance of the three and one-half acres myself. When Maria came up on the weekends, we would plant flowers and such. The neighbors would cheer us on as they passed by. Soon enough, I realized they must have been quite amused, knowing that the deer or groundhogs would devour everything we so enthusiastically planted. I even learned how to shoot a rifle.

I had called an exterminator about some field mice in the house. While he was there, I asked him about getting rid of the groundhogs. They dug so many huge holes in the yard that I was afraid my tractor and I would fall into one, never to be heard of again.

"Lead poisoning" was his response.

"Lead poisoning, what's that?" I asked.

"Bullets," he said, "Get yourself a rifle and shoot them."

I told him I didn't know anything about that. A few hours later, he showed up at my front door with his own personal arsenal. He handed me a .22 rifle, took me out back, and taught me how to use it. Wow! After a half hour lesson, he gave me some extra bullets and told me to hold onto the rifle and get comfortable with it. I was amazed at his kindness. He was White and didn't know me from a hole in the wall, yet he was lending me his rifle. I could have shot up half the town, and his prints would have been on the weapon. Was everyone in the country this trusting?

I practiced with his rifle and eventually went to Walmart to buy my own. Yeah, man, Walmart, life in the country, eh? In no time, I became quite adept at shooting groundhogs. After a kill shot, I would let the groundhog remain for a day or so, allowing rigor mortis to set in, and then I would shovel up the body and dump it in the woods. That was until I noticed a growing coyote population near my house, attracted by the free and easy food. The groundhogs soon became the lesser of two evils. I continued to play with my rifle from time to time, until I learned one day, how deadly it really was.

It was during the spring of 1997, I was stressed. My niece, Candice, then fifteen, was living with me and was still incessantly demanding attention. The disability insurance company had detectives following me and lurking in the woods near my house, which was quite disconcerting. In addition, while adapting to my new life, there was still all my "stuff" that I hadn't dealt with or resolved. As usual, there were deer running around the property. Well, maybe I can't control my niece or the insurance company, but I can surely keep the deer from taking over my property and eating everything, right? I got my gun.

When I fired a few warning shots in the sky, the deer just looked at me as if to say, "girlfriend please." So I shot a little closer to their heads. They turned, looked at me again, and this time they seemed to smirk. The audacity. I pointed my rifle and aimed, hoping to whiz a bullet right by its ear, but I had forgotten about distance and velocity. There was a thud. Panic flooded my heart. I had shot one, and it wasn't hunting season. I could just see the townsfolk forming a lynching party and the state troopers toting me off to prison (can't have this crazy Black woman running around town with a rifle). All I could hope was that the deer hobbled into the woods and died there. Then no one would know it was me. I looked around the grounds and found it lying near my pond. It appeared to be shot in the hip. I made several calls to family and friends for advice (and in case I went missing). Finally, I called Joe, the exterminator, who introduced me to guns in the first place. He told me that I must kill the animal for humanitarian purposes. I could not, and I asked him if he would kill it and remove it from my property. He implored me to kill it, but I really didn't have the heart. He agreed to come the following morning.

I went out to the deer, apologized, and threw it a couple of apples as kind of like a last supper. She looked terrified, as if to say, "First the chick shoots me, and now she's trying to pelt me with apples! Please miss, just leave me alone, and let me die in peace." I was so sorry. I stashed my rifle in the rear of the closet and went down to the city to distance myself from the scene of the crime. All I could think about is, what if that had been my neighbor's little son. I very seldom pick up my rifle anymore, no matter how frustrated or stressed or out of control I might feel. One major lesson I learned from my niece's yearlong stay with me is that I can't control anyone's actions but my own. That lesson has been invaluable, and I continue to be reminded of it by others from time to time.

In 1996, after suffering with extremely heavy menstrual bleeding for almost eight years, I underwent my first and hopefully, only major surgery. At the age of thirty-four, I had been diagnosed with fibroid tumors in my uterus and endured the chronic pain, until it was intolerable. The bleeding and cramping became progressively worse with each passing year. So much so, that I was bleeding more often than I wasn't. The doctors I consulted wanted to treat my condition conservatively with birth control pills. They didn't want to give me a hysterectomy, considering my relatively young age. Finally, at the age of forty-two, I became adamant, "Look man, if you saw the blood that comes out of me, you would know, no pill is going to stop this." My doctor agreed to schedule the surgery.

In preparation for my surgery, I began to donate blood in case it was needed during the surgery. I didn't want to take the chance of getting someone's *tainted* blood. I never had surgery before or had even been hospitalized, but I worked in the field long enough to know the potential dangers. I told the doctor to take out only what needed to be removed. If the ovaries and cervix are fine, leave them. Get in and get out.

Because of the bleeding, I was anemic and had to build up the iron in my blood before they could perform the procedure. While awaiting my surgical date, I received a letter from the lab. In huge print it said, "YOUR BLOOD IS BEING DESTROYED. DO NOT EVER DONATE BLOOD AGAIN." *What?* Upon further reading, it stated that I had hepatitis B and hepatitis C. I didn't really pay it much mind, thinking that most medical professionals are exposed to hepatitis at one time or another, no big deal. I was more concerned with the issue at hand of undergoing surgery.

As the day of my hospitalization approached, I began to get a bit apprehensive. No, I was terrified. I have major trust issues and was about to put my life in the hands of strangers who would knock me out, slice me open, and gut me like some livestock. Oh my goodness! As badly as I wanted the surgery and needed to stop the bleeding, I was not ready to die.

I prayed on a daily basis those days and read the Bible regularly. One morning while praying, I got my answer. It was not the surgeon in whom I needed to put my trust, it was God. Believing if He brought me all this way, through everything I had overcome so far, He wasn't going to leave me now. I was more at peace with the whole idea of surgery knowing God had me.

The morning of the surgery, lying in the pre-op area surrounded by salivating interns, I almost made a frantic dash for the nearest exit. One intern began poking me with a needle attached to the sedation. After a few pokes I screamed at him to get away from me, and I moved to get off the table. The poor guy nearly jumped out of his mask and gown. Almost immediately, a more seasoned anesthesiologist entered the room. I was relieved when I saw an older, more experienced looking doctor. As he prepared to inject me with the anesthesia, I asked him how long I would be under, to which he replied, "It could be an hour; it could be forever; you would never know the difference." I guess he resented the way I treated his intern. Anyway, he proceeded to put me under right away before I could flee. Obviously, Praise God, I survived the surgery, interns and all.

Following the surgery, I felt better and stronger than ever before. By the second week, I was doing sit-ups and painting my pool house. Not having a uterus was the best thing that could ever happen to me. How we women suffer so. Ironically, in my joy of being released from my bondage of bleeding, there was also the pain of deprivation. You see, although I had years before resigned myself to the fact that I would not have any children, when *I could not* have any children, I was devastated and completely unprepared for my feeling of utter loss!

Around the age of thirty-five, I had given serious

consideration as to whether or not I was going to have a child. It would have to have been then or never. I wasn't in a relationship with a man and was not looking to be in one, so the idea of adoption became increasingly engaging. In contemplating adoption versus giving birth, I began to lean towards adoption. My reasoning was thus: the only advantage to actually birthing a child would be based purely in vanity. This child would be of *my* blood, so it would have some of my characteristics, perhaps my intelligence or looks or personality. In essence, it would be *of* me.

Then I thought about the many children in the world already born who needed love and care, children I could love just as well as if they were from me, because my love would make any child my child. Also, intentionally bringing a baby into this troubled world hardly seemed fair to the child. So, adoption looked to be the better of the two options. And I wouldn't have to go through all the discomfort and disfiguration of a pregnancy, although the prospect of not having a period for nine months was very appealing.

So then the question became, do I really want to raise a child? Do I really want to commit the rest of my life to another human being? I decided the wise thing to do was to first join the Big Sisters organization, make a part-time commitment to a child in need, and see how that went. It proved to be a wise decision.

The first weekend that I was supposed to meet my "little sister," I remember lying in bed with dread. After working all week, the last thing I felt like doing was entertaining some nine-year-old kid, but I did it with a good attitude. Because her mother had passed away, my little sister was living with her grandmother and brothers. She and Grandma became part of my family, and to this day, my little sister and I are in touch. However, I did decide that raising a child at that time in my life was not something to which I wanted to commit.

There was too much other stuff going on, working, partying, not to mention the "other" issues, which had not fully presented themselves as yet.

After my hysterectomy, I became very sensitive to relationships between mother and child, especially mother and daughter. The most beautiful sight to me would be to see mothers and daughters of any age together. I could look into the faces of middle-aged women and their elderly mothers and see the mutual resolute love and appreciation they had established over the years. Watching young mothers with baby girls collecting shells on the beach, brought tears to my eyes and a smile to my face in the same heartfelt moment. I missed my own mother and the conversations I would never have with her. I missed my unborn daughter and the love we would never be able to share. I cried for little Melanie and the childhood she could never reclaim, and I cried for old, barren Melanie and the mother she would never be. The one label I would never have is Mommy, although recently while playing a game with my great nieces and nephew, the five-year-old called me Mama, and it so touched my heart.

Yes, the option of adoption was still available. But I didn't really desire to be a mother. I was just melodramatically mourning the fact that I couldn't give birth to my own child. In fact, years later in 2002, I almost adopted a child while visiting in South Africa. Horrified by the news that men were raping babies because they were told that sex with a virgin would cure their AIDS, I felt it was crucial to save at least one baby. By the time I returned to the U.S. and seriously thought about it, I decided I was way too old and didn't really want to sacrifice my final years raising a child. I did feel badly about that.

The issue of motherhood so enveloped me in self-pity that I even found myself crying during diaper commercials on TV. That's when I knew I needed to get a grip. My depression lasted just long enough to truly appreciate motherhood in all its wondrous, complex, elusive dynamics: the love, the disappointments, the rivalries, the resentments, the reconciliations, and the unbreakable and sometimes unbearable bond between mother and daughter.

Being a mother is the most difficult, demanding, often thankless, but the most fulfilling, and utmost important blessing that can be entrusted to a woman. It's a responsibility that never ends, sometimes not even after death. Directly or indirectly, we attribute most of our failures or successes to our mothers. When one goes to therapy, invariably, the first relationship we focus on is our relationship with our mother.

And yes, mothers are very influential in our lives and how we develop as human beings. But moms often get a bum rap. When do we start taking responsibility for our own lives? How are we at fifty still blaming our issues and inadequacies on something that happened when we were *five*? When is it time to let go of the past, to be fully accountable for our present, and mindfully, prayerfully plan for our future?

Someone once used the analogy of a car to our lives: the windshield is large, the rear view mirror is small because it's more important to see where we are going than to see where we have been. Yes, it is vital to understand how we got to where we are, but it shouldn't be used as an excuse for being less than we can be.

Now, those whose mothers are alive and still have ongoing relationships with them could either be blessed or cursed, depending upon their relationship. Please don't misunderstand. But a very curious thing happened to me after my mother died. I'm not sure exactly when I first encountered this feeling, how long after my mom's death, but at some point, there was a certain feeling of freedom, of liberation. Like, now I could come into my own. Not that my mother had been controlling or domineering in any way, but she always had an influence. My life was never quite my own.

I'm sure many of you can identify with what I'm trying to say, should you allow yourself to be honest. Most likely, if Mommy and I had more time, I would have come into my own despite her influence. It's a process, I guess. Perhaps, if she had lived long enough, I would have been able to confront her about the ways she had failed me. I could have told her how I grew up feeling unprotected and unworthy.

Possibly, if she had lived long enough, she could have filled in the gaps in my soul. But then again, if she had lived longer, I might not have ever acknowledged that there was a hole in my soul. And I may never have slain the beast. Remember, you cannot conquer what you don't confront, and you can't confront what you don't identify.

For those of you who are fortunate enough to still have your mothers, appreciate them. Embrace the opportunity you have to express your love, and your disappointments and hurts. Then graciously, cut her some slack! What I realized— how I finally made peace with my mother's seeming insufficiencies—is that she had done the best that she could at any given time. No mother in her right mind or heart, intentionally sets out to hurt her child. Whatever she is doing, however she is doing it, she's doing the best that *she* can at that particular time in *her* life. All we can do is our best and pray to our heavenly Father to help us heal and grow and understand and forgive.

Me, Mommy, Cliff & Carla

ALL YOU NEED IS LOVE

I started investing in real estate in 1992 when Maria and I first got together. She was a savvy realtor, and the first property that I bought, a five family brownstone, in Bedford Park, Bronx, New York was through her. It had been illegally set up as a rooming house and was quite profitable, which is what attracted me to the property, despite the risks and complications. A few years later, I expanded my empire and purchased another property, a twenty-six unit building in the "hood" or ghetto area of the Bronx. It was a beautiful building, and with Maria as the broker and much persistence, I acquired it at a very good price. The only drawback was the neighborhood. Drugs and guns and the folks that use them dominated the streets. With Maria's help, I rose to the challenge of owning and managing the apartment building. We were good partners. Initially it was exciting, but I soon discovered I much preferred procuring properties to managing them, especially in New York City. The tenants were a pain in the rear, and they had all the rights. When you rent an apartment to someone in the city, you better investigate them well because you are just about married to them once they have been in *your* building for more than thirty days. One tenant I will never forget is Lucy Abere.

I hadn't had the building too long, and my only vacancy

was the basement apartment, a nice sized, two-bedroom unit. When I interviewed Lucy, she seemed a bit rough around the edges but harmless enough. She was an Hispanic woman in her early forties, with bleached blonde hair and a slight lisp. I was a little apprehensive about renting her the apartment, something didn't seem quite right, but after all, it was the hood, a basement apartment, she had the money, and I was a bit naïve and inexperienced at being a landlord.

Maria seemed to think she was okay, so what the heck. Lucy had a teenage son and daughter, who, unbeknownst to me at the time, didn't attend school. She described them, though, as good kids. I later found out her fifteen-year-old daughter had a child, who also lived with them. Well, that first month's rent was the only rent I saw for months! After a couple of months of excuses, I began the eviction process, and what a process it is. First, you engage an attorney, who files the necessary papers with the courts and then engages a process server to serve your tenant. It usually takes a month or two before you even get to court. Then it gets tricky. What I hadn't realized when I rented the apartment to Lucy was that she was what they call a "professional tenant." She had probably been through this process a hundred times and knew the game very well. And so the games began.

We went back and forth to court, and each time the judge allowed her more time, so I could effect the repairs of the tenant-inflicted damages to the apartment. Then the judge would grant more time to her for some agency to kick in and pay her back rent. This costly process went on for months.

Just when we were about at the end, when she was out of excuses, when the judge was out of "orders to show cause," and just when I was about to be free, a new character showed up on the scene, her husband, Tony Abere. He apparently winterered on the island—Rikers Island, that is, New York City's largest correctional facility. Things really got interesting after his arrival.

Although he was Puerto Rican, Tony had a big, wild Afro. He was thin and brown, with a heavy Hispanic accent. What a pair. Tony was HIV positive, so upon his release from prison, it seemed he had quite a few entitlements. One program was actually going to pay his wife's back rent in addition to all future rents.

Unbelievable! When my brother was dying, I couldn't get DAS (Department of Aids Services) to pay his rent. I paid it. And Cliff, at least, worked before he became ill. In any case, their rent was paid, and now they were home free (literally) to wreak havoc in *my* building.

The drug dealing from the basement apartment began almost immediately. Of course, I notified the police. I also joined the "clean halls" program and whatever else to ensure the integrity and safety of my building and its tenants, all to no avail. The Aberes had taken over the building or at least the basement and alleyway. They held bizarre religious rites that entailed slaughtering pigs in my alleyway. They intimidated the building super, especially when during one of their outrageous religious ceremonies, they would answer their door naked, covered in pig's blood. Knocking on their door to inform them of their infractions, only provoked curses and threats. I dreaded going to that building.

One day, when Maria and I went to check the property, Lucy and Tony were outside.

"Dere they are, dere they are!" Lucy began to shout and point at us. "Dere go da ones that keep calling the police!" She was calling to someone down the street.

As we entered the building, Tony approached us in a threatening manner. "Ju know," his accent made his words almost indecipherable. "I don't understand why ju keep harassing my family like dis. What, ju don' like us 'cause we got a life?"

We didn't know to whom Lucy was calling, but we rang our tenants' doorbells until someone let us in, and then we called the police. After about half an hour when the police didn't come, we gathered our composure and went about the business of the building. Upon exiting the building, Tony approached me, "Yeah, da police came and went. Now what you gonna do?"

I brushed past him to check on Maria, who was talking to some guy in a gold hooptie van. (A hooptie van in the hood is an old, beat up gangster van with dark tinted windows, probably used for drive by shootings.) The driver was Hispanic with gold teeth that were bedazzled with emeralds or rubies or something or other. Viciously peering at us from the rear of the van was a Rottweiller.

The driver then informed me, "I was just telling Ma, I run these streets and you need to stop calling the police. Drugs was here before you came here, and they'll be here after you leave, so all you doin' is upsetting the balance of power."

What the hell! I got thugs schooling me on the geopolitics of the ghetto in addition to threatening me.

"Look man," I replied, "you run the streets, and your investment is out here on the streets. My investment is in my building, and I can't have people selling drugs in it. It's bad for my business."

"Ain't nobody sellin' drugs in your buildin', Ma." He seemed to be getting irritated.

I could see it was time for me to practice a little diplomacy. "Cool man, you run the block, and you say that no one is selling drugs in my building, then I'll leave that to you. As long as no one is selling drugs in my building, then we don't have a problem, all right?" I held out my hand. He shook it. Maria and I got in my car. His van was parked parallel to my car, blocking it from the side, and his boys were parked in front and behind us. Maria reached in her bag and pulled out a pad.

"I'm going to take down their license plate numbers," she said with unbelievably naïve enthusiasm.

"Put the pad down, put the pen down, put your head down, and let's drive off this block alive." I was exasperated.

All I wanted was to get to the nearest liquor store and get home safely. I was so frustrated because I felt as if I had lost all control of my building, and for someone as controlling as myself, it was almost unbearable. I began to dream of the Aberes, that I was in the basement, clubbing them to death. This became a recurrent dream. I hated the Aberes! And I hated the fact that I hated anyone. Moreover, in addition to torturing my days, I hated that they invaded my dreams at night. I began to pray for God to get them out of my life, out of my thoughts and dreams. Because it gave me peace and strength, I began to read the 27th Psalm every day: "The Lord is my light and my salvation, whom shall I fear? The Lord is the stronghold of my life, of whom shall I be afraid? When evil men advance against me to devour my flesh, when my enemies and foes attack me, they will stumble and fall ... Wait for The Lord; be strong and take heart and wait for The Lord." I read it every day for months.

Finally, as summer's end approached, it was time for Tony and the boys (They had some sons who also entered the scene.) to again winter on "the island." Even though Tony was incarcerated, DAS continued to pay the rent. I called them, and protested, "How is it that as a taxpayer, I am supporting him in prison, and also supporting his family? It just doesn't make any sense to me."

They tried to convince me that it was legitimate, but I wasn't accepting it. Hell, I might as well start dealing drugs. It seems I would have more rights and benefits. Anyway, when I threatened to contact my congressman and have the matter thoroughly investigated, the payments stopped.

We began the eviction process again with the damages, the repairs, and the holdovers. Lucy had complained of a hole in her wall, one of many stall tactics, so I went to investigate. Her apartment was filthy. Although it was the middle of the day, each bedroom had a mattress with people asleep, drunk, drugged, or something, and amidst this filth and depravity, was her six-year-old granddaughter. When I asked Lucy what happened to the wall, she replied, "Well Meladie, I was trying to open a coconut with dis hammer, and when I couldn't crack it I got mad and threw the hammer into the wall."

All I could say was, "Hmmm." I wasn't angry. I wasn't fearful. Lucy seemed like a child.

I sat down in the living room and beckoned her granddaughter to come to me. Audrey was her name. I asked her if she prayed. She told me that she did. I asked her what did she pray, and she proceeded to recite, "Now I lay me down to sleep, I pray..." She stumbled through the words, so we said them together, "the Lord my soul to keep. If I should die before I wake, I pray the Lord my soul to take." I was touched. Perhaps it was my negative experiences as a child that made me more sensitive to Audrey. She no longer seemed like this prematurely grown, rude child with a womanly strut. She was just a baby, surrounded by depravity and ignorance. What must she see and hear on a daily basis? I called Lucy into the living room and told her that I would give her three thousand dollars if she moved within a month. She seemed agreeable.

While saying my prayers the next morning, I thought about the little girl, Audrey, Lucy's granddaughter. I became concerned for her, living in that household. To me, the worst thing someone could do is harm a child, and she seemed to live in harm's way. I prayed for her, for her safety, for her childhood.

Well, a month went by. Lucy reported that she could find no other place to live, so our little legal dance continued. Again, I thought I had her gone. During the court session, I sat next to my expensive attorney, and she sat next to her daughter. It seemed things were finally going my way, but just as I was about to breathe a sigh of relief, Lucy pulled out some checks to present to the judge. I couldn't believe my eyes! Talk about nine lives. The judge took the checks from the court officer, looked at them, gave them back to the officer and directed him to give them to me.

I quickly spoke up, "Uh, I don't want the money, your Honor. I just want them gone."

"Take the checks, landlord," was her reply.

"Uh, but your Honor," my voice quavering.

"Take the checks, landlord!" Tears rolled down my face as I grievously "took the checks." I felt so defeated. Lucy just smiled.

The checks she gave me in court covered the back rent and the current rent due, but she was soon in arrears again. Again, we went through the whole process, months of back and forth to court. Finally, the day came! Lucy had run out of time and resources. The eviction was scheduled, and the marshals were at her door. Soon I would be free. I was driving through the Bronx on my way upstate, singing songs of joy and praise as I anticipated getting champagne to celebrate Lucy's long awaited departure. My cell phone rang, rarely a good thing. It was the marshal's office.

"Ms. Lewis?" asked a very macho cop sounding voice.

"Yes."

"This is Marshal Damonte. I'm at Lucy Abere's apartment."

"Yes," I replied, uneasily. "Is she out?"

"No Ma'am, I can't evict her."

"What do you mean you can't evict her?" I couldn't breathe.

"There is a wheelchair and an oxygen tank in her living room which she claims is hers. She's disabled. I can't legally evict her from the apartment, Ma'am. Sorry." He said this so matter-of-factly. Did he not realize his words were like a knife in my heart? I could have driven my car right off the Bronx River Parkway, through the fencing to the ravine below. "But wait, what am I supposed to do now?" I asked, desperately.

"You'll have to go back to court."

Un-freaking believable! My champagne celebration turned into a night of quaffing cognac. It seemed I would never be rid of these people.

Shortly after that, Tony and the crew were back on the streets doing business as usual. I kept praying, not only for the child, but for Lucy, too. I began to wonder what Lucy's childhood must have been like for her to become the adult that she was. I began to have compassion, even love, for her and her family. The nightmares of clubbing them to death in the basement were gone. The fear of entering my own building was gone. I realized there must be a lesson in this somewhere, and when God is ready, this too shall pass.

During this time, Lucy claimed she slipped and fell in her bathroom and brought a million dollar lawsuit against me. I informed the insurance company that her claim was bogus, and I would cooperate in any way possible to fight it. Enough is enough, already. While sitting in the attorney's outer office waiting to give my deposition, Tony and I got into conversation. He was looking as wild and as malefic as usual, but amazingly, we were very cordial to each other. We spoke about current affairs or sports or something innocuous, and although I was a bit annoyed that their little shenanigans were again costing me time and money, it was okay. During our conversation, I mentioned to him the deal I offered Lucy while he was incarcerated. It was obvious to me, after over two years of trying, I wasn't going to be rid of them via the legal system, so I needed to be creative.

"Hey, Tony," I nonchalantly brought into the conversation, "If you guys move out within a month, I'll give you five thousand dollars." I figured having just been released from prison, he would need seed money to start his business again. Not that I wanted to fund his illegal activities, but they needed to go.

"Really, Melanie?" His eyes opened wide.

"Really, Tony." It wasn't that I had excess money to give away like that, but I would probably end up spending at least that much in legal fees anyway as the years ensued. Although I was no longer in distress about their presence in my building, it was preferable that they be gone. There was no more hatred, no more fear. Love and concern for a child had brought me to a much higher place. I understood and even forgave the Aberes their offenses. They were merely surviving the best way they knew how, the only way they knew how. It really had nothing to do with me, personally.

A few years ago, I read an excellent book *The Four Agreements* by Miguel Ruiz. To summarize, the four agreements are: 1. Always do your best, 2. Be impeccable with your word, 3. Don't make assumptions, and 4. Don't take anything personally. I try to honor these agreements, as I find it is a beneficial practice, especially "Don't take anything personally," which we almost always do. Reality is, how people treat us and behave toward us has really very little to do with us. Most of us operate from the perspective of ME/I, and what we manifest on the outside is merely a reflection of what is happening on the inside.

Anyway, what the enemy sent for my destruction, God turned around for good. I understood what it truly meant to love one's enemies, a lesson I'll not soon forget. "There is no fear in love. But perfect love casts out fear" (1 John 4:18). The

Aberes were put in my life to teach me this principle. I've had several occasions to test it, and it proves itself to be true again and again. It was time for us to end. The Aberes had served their purpose in my life and in my spiritual growth. It was time to expend my energy, time, and attention on other things. Tony did find another apartment. He turned in the keys to my attorney and collected his check for five thousand dollars—the Aberes were gone within the month.

Whenever I've had to deal with someone who was unpleasant or hateful in some way, someone who evoked less than desirable feelings in me, or who frightened or angered me (and anger is just another manifestation of fear), I sought to find some place in my heart where I could attain some level of love for him or her. And every time, the love overcame the fear.

Now I ain't gonna lie, this practice does not come easily or instinctively. Sometimes, I forget the secret and allow a situation to make me angry or anxious. Sometimes, I really have to pray hard to even want to get to that place of love. But these days, my peace is paramount to my survival, and when I am angry or anxious, it disrupts my peace to the point of physical pain. They say love hurts. Well, I think hate hurts much more.

I truly experienced the prodigious power of love. Not the romantic love we all so desperately, endlessly seem to seek but spiritual love, Godly love. We write songs about love and books about love. We make movies about love, talk about it, blog about it, cry about it. We love shoes and cars and sports teams and even fried chicken (one of my great loves). Yet most of us haven't the slightest clue what true love really is. The word lightly rolls off our tongues without us recognizing the magnitude of the concept. Even our dictionaries only narrowly define the word in its passionate or sexual connotations.

The Greek language actually has four words for love. *Eros* is defined as a sexual kind of love, from which we derive the word *erotic*. Next, we have *agape*, which is more of a godly love. Agape love isn't a feeling as much as it is an action, a behavior based on the command of Jesus for us to "love one another, just as I have loved you" (John 13:34), like the love I practiced with the Aberes. When God sent His son to die on the cross, it surely wasn't pleasurable to Him. He did it out of agape love for us. "For God so loved the world that He gave his only begotten Son that whosoever believes in him should not perish but have eternal life" (John. 3:16). Now, I'm not comparing my relationship with the Aberes to Jesus's sacrifice on the cross. Heaven forbid. But you get the idea, right? Agape love requires we do the right thing even though it may feel wrong.

For instance, a few years ago a friend of mine asked to borrow five thousand dollars for some sort of business investment that she believed would be profitable. It didn't really sound like a lucrative deal to me, and my *spirit* wasn't really feeling it. As a businesswoman, my policy on lending money is, don't lend what you can't afford to lose. Surely, I was not prepared to lose five thousand dollars. However, I was preoccupied and wasn't really interested in hearing all the details of her business endeavor. She and her family had been struggling for years with one thing or another, and if I could help them get ahead of the game in some way, well it was my Christian duty to help my sister in Christ. I recalled the Biblical reference regarding not denying those in need when it is in your power to help. Bottom line: My friend knew me well enough to know that I wanted my money paid back in full. I loaned her the money.

Always trust your spirit's promptings, even when they may seem to contradict what you have read. One must develop discernment through the Holy Spirit, which takes relationship and time. So...the deadline for the loan repayment came and went: no money. Now this particular friend had been in financial distress before, and I had helped her and her family on several previous occasions, but to me business is business, and a loan is business! She did pay me a little here and there, perhaps totaling two thousand dollars over the course of a year. But then the Holy Spirit spoke to me. My friend and her family were still having financial trials, and it was clear that it was a painful effort for her to make any payments to me, so I was moved to forgive the loan. I didn't want to. I wanted my money. The Lord told me to forget it, and I was like, "But, Lord, if she couldn't have paid it back, she shouldn't have borrowed it. This will be a good lesson for her." But God insisted that I forgive it, and so I did. It *hurt*!

I think I was mostly angry with myself for not following my *spirit's* promptings to not give her the loan at all. But in my heart, I knew that I did not want to cause my friend any additional grief or stress, and I knew that the loan hanging over her head was stressful because she did not want to lose my friendship. Now, truth be told, I can't say I will ever lend her any money again. But the following year, she was in need. Through the love of God, I was able to generously and graciously help her, and it was truly my pleasure, agape love.

The third kind of love found in the Greek language is *philo*, which is more like a friendship love, a fondness or special interest in someone or something. And finally, the fourth Greek word for love is *storge*, which is a love of family or a devotional love.

Anyway, life in the country continued. No eros to speak of, but I was learning about agape, was thankful for the philos in my life, and continued to cherish my storge.

GAY AND GODLY

All during my convalescence in the country, my relationship with God continued to grow, and I came to know Him as my Father. I attended a Baptist church for a few years. The choir was excellent, though the pastor didn't move me much. Fortunately, there were guest pastors who were better at teaching, so occasionally the sermons were inspirational. But mostly at this particular church, it was through the singing gospel of praise and worship that I communed with The Lord.

One Sunday, I brought Maria, my partner, to church with me. I was beginning to feel as if I finally had a church home, and I wanted to share it with her. Well, that Sunday the pastor's sermon turned into a homophobic harangue, ending in his repeated screaming, "I'm a MAN, and I like *women*." It was frightening and humiliating and very disappointing.

I knew the Baptist church didn't embrace homosexuality, but never did I anticipate such blatant hatred. I was completely devastated. I couldn't even get up to walk out. Plus, I was probably afraid I'd be stoned on the way out and not in the good way. Needless to say, I never went back again. I was already in relationship with God, so the pastor's condemnation of my lifestyle did not affect my relationship with My Father. Too often, we are negatively influenced by religion or religious people, when it is not about religion at all but about relationship. As described in Acts, when the church was initially established it was not divided into subsections of Baptists, Episcopals, Catholics, Lutherans, etc. It was established as the body of Christ. Religion was created by man. Jesus came, so we could have a relationship with His Father, Our Father.

I've come to notice that a lot of gay people reject a relationship with The Lord because they have been rejected by the church, or so-called Christians, or religious people. To my gay sisters and brothers, I want to say right here and now, don't ever let anyone deny you a relationship with YOUR Heavenly Father. And He is just that: Our Father who art in heaven. As I previously mentioned, when I first started attending church as an adult, I always felt less than, like everyone else was so holy, and I was so lowly. Now that I am a seasoned believer in Jesus the Christ and the sacrifice that He made for me, for Us, I do not allow anyone to judge me nor do I judge myself. Galatians 3:26 informs us, "You are all sons of God through faith in Christ Jesus, for all of you who were baptized into Christ have clothed yourselves with Christ. There is neither Jew nor Greek, slave nor free, male nor female, for you are all one in Christ Jesus."

Don't let anyone deny you your birthright! James 4:8 tells us, "Come near to God and He will come near to you." Your Father wants to be in relationship with you. He wants to bless you and love you and give you peace. It is a lifelong process of spiritual growth and evolution. No one has achieved perfection, and no one has the right to judge anyone. Jesus Himself tells us, "Judge not, lest ye be judged."

Our Father created us to first be in relationship with Him. The Bible tells us to have faith. It is defined in the book of Hebrews as "being sure of what we hope for and certain of what we do not see." We, even the non-believers among us, practice faith all the time. We have faith that when we sit in a chair, it will hold our weight. We have faith that when we open a faucet, water will come out. We have faith that with the press of a button, our TV will transport us just about anywhere our minds desire to go. We don't know how, and we don't care. We just have faith that on any particular night, we can go "Dancing With the Stars," get lost in the suspense of "Scandal," or cachinnate with the "Modern Family." We can be thrilled or chilled, laugh, cry and have all kinds of virtual experiences.

Think about it, though. We have faith in all these things, all these human creations. So who created *us*, the greatest creation of all? Anyone with even infinitesimal intelligence can clearly see that we are too magnificently, wonderfully, gloriously made to have been an accident, an aberration of nature. Look at our universe. To me, it's much more difficult to believe that it just exploded out of nothingness than to believe that a force more incredible than I could possibly fathom created all of this for me and created me for Himself. My Father!

The Bible tells us, "And without faith it is impossible to please God, because anyone who comes to Him must believe that He exists, and that He rewards those who earnestly seek Him" (Hebrews 11:6). I look at it this way: If the atheists and agnostics are right and there is no God, no Jesus or heaven and hell, well, I'm still blessed because I have spent my life striving to grow spiritually, to be a better person, and to walk in peace and love. I mean, you're not losing anything but have so much to gain. But if the non-believers are wrong and there is a God and a heaven and hell, well, they will have an eternity to regret it.

Don't get me wrong. I don't choose to believe in God in order to escape hell. In fact, I don't give much thought either way to the afterlife. I'm more concerned with the quality of life that I experience now. I chose to believe in God and to love Him because he believed in and loved me first. Time and time again, He courted me and proved His faithfulness to me. That's why I now love Him. He is the only Father I have ever truly known, and I do love Him, even though, at times I find it difficult to be obedient (more times than I would care to acknowledge).

Perhaps it is because when I was a child, I had no earthly father of substance with whom I could have established such a relationship, no paternal references from which to draw upon. My Heavenly Father knows that I am a work in progress, and He is merciful and forgiving. But He is no fool and will not be mocked. We are held accountable for what we know. So, for all of you out there who fall short (which is what sin means: falling short of the mark), I implore you, don't be fooled or intimidated or shamed into believing you are unworthy of a relationship with God. Truth is, we *all* fall short. And don't fall into the trap of delaying seeking Him until you are doing better. He meets us where we are, no matter how high or how low we think we are. So just open your heart. No, open your mouth, and ask God to open your heart to receive His love. Then open a Bible, one you can understand, like a New International Version or something with plain words. Don't be intimidated.

The Old Testament tells stories of people like you and me, God's people who are flawed but still loved. In the first book alone, Genesis, you have brother killing brother, drunkenness, incest, depravity, and all sorts of goings on. When I first started reading the Old Testament, it reminded me of a soap opera. Maybe try Proverbs first. There are thirty-one chapters in Proverbs, one for each day of the month. Basically, they are just wise sayings, so read a chapter a day for each corresponding day. You are sure to get one or two words of wisdom from just three minutes of your time.

Need some tips on how to pray? Try Psalms, a book of

prayers and songs, many of which were written by King David, a mighty man of God, who was also an adulterer and murderer. In Psalms, David vacillates between joy and praise and deep depression. By today's standards, he would probably be considered bipolar. Even God was unpleasantly surprised at how bad people were. Genesis 6:5 states, "The Lord saw how great man's wickedness on the earth had become, and that every inclination of the thoughts of his heart was only evil all the time. The Lord was grieved that he had made man on the earth, and his heart was filled with pain. So the Lord said, 'I will wipe mankind, whom I have created, from the face of the earth...for I am grieved that I have made them.'" Fortunately for us, one man, Noah, found favor in the eyes of the Lord thus, the story of Noah's Ark.

The first four books of the New Testament are called The Gospels or The Good News. They give us a well-rounded account of Jesus's life and teachings as told by four of his disciples. Just in case some of you are not familiar with Jesus, He is God's son, the second person of the Holy Trinity (The Father, The Son and The Holy Spirit), who became a man, the only man without sin. He was crucified to redeem us from our sins, and He rose from the dead. I am not a Bible scholar, and I don't want to go too deep. You will understand as you grow in your walk with Him.

Following the Gospel is the book of Acts, which gives an account of the birth of the church (body of Christ) and the coming of the Holy Spirit. The remainder of the New Testament is basically comprised of God-inspired letters, written by the apostle Paul and Jesus's disciples. Most of the New Testament was written by a murderer. Yes, Paul, who as Saul of Tarsus before he came to know Jesus, used to persecute and murder Christians. On his way to Damascus to continue his persecutions, a light from heaven flashed around him rendering him blind. Jesus confronted him and then sent him on his way to the city. He remained blinded for three days until scales fell from his eyes, and he was converted, filled with the Holy Spirit. You will find the story in Acts, chapter 9.

Some of Jesus's disciples were imprisoned, so they're ex-cons, right? In fact, many of Paul's letters were written from his prison cell. So please, never, ever feel less than. Your heavenly Father loves you so and wants to be part of your life. The Bible is truly a living book. Each time you read it, you will get new revelations and insights. As you begin to open your heart and mind to God, He will give you understanding and wisdom. Draw near to Him, and He *will* draw near to you.

To my Christian brothers and sisters, I quote John 8:7, "Let he who is without sin, cast the first stone." Don't get me wrong. I'm not implying that same sex relationships are sinful just as not all heterosexual relationships are without sin. In fact, Romans 3:23 tells us, "for all have sinned and fall short of the glory of God." So don't be hypocritical, you know Jesus doesn't like hypocrites!

But on the subject of homosexuality, I do not purport that all healthy, same sex relationships are either condoned or condemned by God. I would not begin to be so presumptuous as to pretend I know what God expects of each individual or of whose relationships He does and does not approve. We seek relationship with Him, so He can communicate to us what He expects of us individually and collectively. In Ecclesiastes 7:20, Solomon tells us, "There is not a righteous man on earth, who does what is right and never sins."

I personally stand on Romans 14:

> Accept him whose faith is weak, without passing judgment on disputable matters. One man's faith allows him to eat everything, but another

man whose faith is weak eats only vegetables. The man who eats everything must not look down on him who does not, and the man who does not eat everything must not condemn the man who does, for God has accepted him. Who are you to judge someone else's servant? To his own master he stands or falls. And he will stand, for the Lord is able to make him stand. One man considers one day more sacred than another, another man considers every day alike. Each one should be fully convinced in his own mind. He, who regards one day as special, does so to the Lord. He who eats meat eats to the Lord for he gives thanks to God. For none of us lives to himself alone and none of us dies to himself alone. If we live we live to the Lord and if we die we die to the Lord. So whether we live or die, we belong to the Lord. For this reason, Christ died and returned to life so that He might be the Lord of both the dead and the living. You then, why do you judge your brother? For we will all stand before God's judgment seat. It is written: As surely as I live, says the Lord every knee will bow before me; every tongue will confess to God. So then, each of us will give an account of himself to God. Therefore, let us stop passing judgment on one another. Instead, make up your mind not to put any stumbling block or obstacle in your brother's way. As one who is in the Lord Jesus, I am fully convinced that no food is unclean in itself. But if anyone regards something as unclean, THEN FOR HIM IT IS UNCLEAN. If your brother is distressed because of what you eat, you are no longer acting in love. Do not by your eating destroy your brother for whom Christ died. ***Do not allow what you consider good to be spoken of as evil.*** For the kingdom of God is not a matter of eating and drinking, but of righteousness, joy and peace in the Holy Spirit, because anyone who serves Christ in this way is pleasing to God and approved by men. Let us therefore make every effort to do what leads to peace and to mutual edification. Do not destroy the work of God for the sake of food. All food is clean but it is wrong for a man to eat anything that causes someone else to stumble. It is better not to eat meat or drink wine or do anything else that will cause your brother to fall. So whatever you believe about these things KEEP THEM BETWEEN YOURSELF AND GOD. ***Blessed is the man who does not condemn himself by what he approves.***

So for those of you who view same sex relationships as sinful, YOU should not participate in a same sex relationship.

I believe homosexuality is an easy target for those who preach on sin, because homosexuals are a minority in the church and in society. It is quite easy to condemn an act in which you have no part. The Bible lists many "sins" emphatically. Gluttony is one of them. Although the churches are overflowing with overweight Christians, I have yet to hear a sermon on gluttony. Proverbs 23:2 advises, "Put a knife to your throat if you are given to gluttony." There's a televised minister I occasionally watch whom I call Tom Hate-tee. He could be preaching about the beauty of the sun, the moon, and the stars and then all of a sudden go into a diatribe about homosexuals. The hypocrisy would be funny if it weren't so dangerous. Tom is overweight, but I never heard him preach on gluttony.

Then there are the liars, thieves, adulterers, gossipers, the prideful etc., etc. The list of sins and sinners goes on. Every so-called Christian can claim at least one or two sins on a daily basis. So how does one measure the degree of sin? By the number of times any particular one is mentioned in the Bible? By who mentions it, e.g., Jesus or Paul or John? I guess the worst sins are the ones we personally are not participating in at the moment. So, we choose to attack homosexuality as one of the greatest sins of all. Truth is, Jesus doesn't even mention homosexuality during His ministry here on earth. However, when asked which is the greatest commandment in the law, he replied, "Love the Lord your God with all your heart and all your soul and all your mind. And the second is similar: Love your neighbor as yourself" (Matthew 22:37). The main theme of Jesus's ministry is love. Read your Bibles, people! Statistics show that less than ten percent of Christians read their Bibles regularly. Hmnnn....

I saw a documentary about a growing anti-homosexual movement in Uganda led by a " Christian" pastor and a politician. Throughout the country, they dispersed negative, inaccurate, and hateful propaganda about gays, advocating the death penalty for citizens believed to be homosexual. Uh...isn't one of the ten commandments, "thou shall not kill"? The most frightening thing about the movement was the people's eager willingness to adopt this hatred. It was mind-boggling, because many of these people were poverty stricken, struggling to survive. How do you have time to so adamantly hate someone you don't know or understand? I bet that same pastor and politician won't be heading up a movement to kill all the adulterers.

Ignorance is a very dangerous thing, but I've come to realize it is prevalent right here in America among my brothers and sisters in Christ. Most of them just have no understanding of a homosexual's life. They are ignorant of the hows and whys and whats that we experience when we laboriously make the decision to be true to our own nature. Even the term *homosexual* offends me. There is so much more to a relationship, a love between two consensual adults than sex. In fact, in most loving relationships, sex plays a relatively minor role after the first few years. I am not condemning anyone for their ignorance nor am I proselytizing homosexuality; I want only to promote godly love and mercy.

I can understand how someone who is not homosexual innately would have difficulty comprehending, much less accepting the essence of it all. I can see how some flamboyant gay behavior could be a turn-off and perceived as deviant. Even I have occasionally found some of the behavior and raiment of my fellow gays to be distasteful. Recently, I was at a tea dance (They don't serve tea, but it starts in the afternoon.) given by an LGBT (lesbian, gay, bi-sexual, trans-gender,) organization. There were quite a few old and tired drag queens there, who were poorly impersonating women. One, with five o'clock shadow and hairy arms wore a long blonde wig, a pair of funky looking shorts, a tank top and heels. A few others were similarly dressed. I thought it was frightening and quite frankly a bit disgusting and ridiculous. I tend to be judgmental at times, but I'm working on that. I never said I was perfect. There was even one man there who called himself Sister Sarah. He told me he was a nun in Asia or somewhere. I'm thinking, these guys are demented.

But before I could turn my nose up too high, I had to look at them with my heart. What must these men, who began their lives as boys, what must they have experienced? How much abuse had they been subject to in their lifetimes? I mean not just the run-of-the-mill abuse that we all experience at some time or other in our lives but the additional abuse of those who are brave enough or desperate enough to openly claim and proclaim their variation from the accepted societal norm. (Kindly note, I used the term *variation* and not *deviation*; there's a difference.)

To announce it to family and friends and ultimately to society, how much rejection and ridicule must they have endured? How many hate crimes might they have suffered, long before such acts were even acknowledged as hate crimes? In fact, how often must they have been targeted by their "normal," judgmental, cowardly peers; their classmates; neighbors; and even family and friends? How isolated they must have felt at times, must still feel at times, despite supportive organizations that exist today. I began to look at them differently, like brave soldiers who were willing to endure the battle in order to claim their personal freedom. How courageous they were. How dauntless.

I had the occasion to socialize with these men again. They are actually transsexuals, not drag queens as I had originally thought. (A drag queen is a man who dresses like a woman. A transsexual is someone who believes he or she is in the wrong sexually oriented body and undergoes treatments and procedures to change his or her sex.)

We were at a Black family reunion barbeque. The hostess, who was a lesbian, had invited quite a few of us from the LGBT center. One of the transsexuals had come to the table at which some of my lesbian friends and I were sitting. He was a big, White guy with a blonde ponytail, a French manicure, and a marine tattoo. The manicure and the ponytail were the only feminine characteristics I could see. He had not fully transitioned yet. As far as I was concerned, he was more man than woman. He invited us to join the women's group at the LGBT center, of which he was the head. When he went to get a pen and paper to write down our email addresses, I looked at my friend and asked, "Uh, was that a woman?" She just looked at me, perplexed, shrugged her shoulders, and with the faintest smirk replied, "I don't know." Surmising that he may have felt a bit out of place or alone at the barbeque, when he returned, I invited him to join us. Soon after, another transsexual sat at our table. He seemed to be at about the same stage of his transition, more man than woman.

After a few glasses of wine, the men and I began to talk more intimately about their transsexualism and why they felt the need to transition. They both had been married to women. They both had children, and they both felt like failures as husbands and fathers in the traditional all-American/white picket fence definition. Mary, as he called himself, had joined the Marines, trying to butch up, but he didn't last for very long. Alice said that while trying to maintain a conventional façade, he attempted suicide twice. They were both on hormones but had not yet undergone surgery, so they both still had penises.

Alice was nearest to me, so we began our own conversation.

"So Alice, do you have a partner?"

"No," he said softly. I got the distinct impression that he hadn't had one in a long time. "Most gay men want more butch guys," he continued.

"I would imagine that bisexuals or straight men might be a little abusive to you," I conjectured.

He seemed surprised that I would have that insight and replied, "Yeah, a lot of times they are, and the guys that are married, but sneaking around..." He paused.

"You mean the guys on the down-low (men who claim to be heterosexual but secretly have sex with other men)?" I interjected.

"Yeah, they can be really mean," said Alice. "It's not about love for them or even sex; it's more about dominance and abuse."

I sighed, just vaguely beginning to comprehend the depth of the pain these guys have experienced. I believe it was

Frances Thompson, a poet, who wrote, "We are born in other's pain and perish in our own."

"So, but why transition, Alice? Why not just be an effeminate man?" I asked.

"Because, from the time I was a child I never felt like a male. I always felt as if I were in the wrong body. I didn't understand why I couldn't play with dolls and have tea parties like the rest of the little girls."

"I get it. When I was a little girl, I used to run around the projects in a cowboy hat with a gun and a holster. In addition to my feminine side, I have a very masculine side, and when I was younger and visibly had more testosterone, I thought I should have been a guy. I even had an alter-ego for a while during my adolescence, my big brother Mel. But ultimately, I'm glad to be a woman."

I think I was almost trying to convince him not to go any further, seeing nothing but more pain for him without ultimate resolution or peace. Both these men were at least fifty years old, so what's the point at this stage of the game, I wondered.

Alice, trying to convince me or perhaps himself, calmly but firmly stated, "The first fifty years of my life, I tried to please everybody else. Now I want to please myself. In my spirit and in my heart, I feel as if I am a woman. I want my body to match."

"Okay, so then after you have transitioned, whom would you date? We've already established your pool of men is very shallow."

"Well, I feel closest to women. I would most likely have a lesbian lover," he replied as if it were taken for granted.

"What!" Now, I'm dumbfounded.

My lesbian friend, Debra, enters the conversation, "Well, of course, that's only natural."

"What?" I felt as if I had too much wine and not enough

life experience. What are they talking about? I really couldn't wrap my head around the whole concept of changing one's sex.

Later that afternoon, I was openly admiring a sexy, young, straight woman who was attending the barbeque. Mary, the other transsexual who confirmed that he is bi-sexual, agreed with me about her beauty, but he'd found another young, Black woman at our table even more attractive. We had a conversation earlier about the allure of women of color. Anyway, Mary went on and on about this woman, so I took a photo of them together.

"Mary," I finally had to say, "Wouldn't it be ironic if after all of this, you discovered that you just hadn't met the right woman of color, and that you needn't be transsexual at all?"

He laughed, "Yes, Melanie, it would be truly ironic."

I am not unfamiliar with the judgment and rejection involved with being gay, which is quite the oxymoron in itself as there is usually nothing "gay" about it. Fortunately, my negative experiences were not too often and not very severe, although I was behaving suicidal, for a while, wasn't I? During my college days in Alabama, I was called names along with my 6'2" beautifully flamboyant, gay, male friend Vincent. Vincent is one of the many loved ones whom I lost to AIDS during that seven-year period of deaths in my life.

When I moved to the Bahamas I was often referred to as a "sissy," behind my back of course. It was intimidating at first because the Bahamian culture is not as diverse or tolerant as the culture in New York. I almost behaved as if I had forgotten all I had gone through to claim the right to be who I am. I soon overcame that. People often treat you according to how you project yourself. If you walk with pride and self-acceptance and treat people with respect, you are usually treated accordingly. Often, this is easier said than done. It takes practice. I had my moments of being over the top, gender-wise, exploring my more masculine side in my dress and mannerisms. At times, I felt quite masculine though I never considered a sex change. I used to jokingly say that I was a White male trapped in the body of a Black woman. White, because from the time I was a child, I was educated with and competed with mostly White males and was surrounded by White culture.

I'm glad that I'm a woman, especially a Black woman, particularly a Black, lesbian woman, and most thankfully a Black, lesbian woman of God. I, personally, don't believe in unnecessary cosmetic surgery. I mean, unless you're deformed or mutilated in some way. But obviously, transsexuals do feel deformed in their birth bodies, which is why they undergo onerous, painful, unpredictable procedures and surgeries towards having their sex changed. I recently encountered Mary again. He told me the hormone treatments are affecting his diabetes, and he may have to have some toes amputated.

"Really, why don't you just stop, man?" I asked. "Usually, once a diabetic starts getting amputations, it becomes a progressive process. Your wading pool of prospective partners is already meager. Being a transsexual amputee, ain't gonna be cute! You know what I mean?"

He just dropped his head. "I know," he said.

I was at a Halloween party one night, again at the LGBT center. I was on line for the ladies room, standing behind this beautiful, Caucasian woman. As one of my exes once told me, I'm a sucker for a pretty face, so I decided to make conversation and see where it went. Because it was Halloween, there were a lot of guys in drag and a few transsexuals. It occurred to me it would behoove me to ask this gorgeous woman if she was indeed a woman.

"I am now!" she proudly answered, much to my great disappointment.

I complimented her on her beauty and kept it movin'. Later that evening, I saw her at the bar with her boyfriend. She was squatting down in front of him making lewd gestures.

I tapped her on the shoulder, and said, "Get up!"

She just looked at me from her squat position.

"Get up!" I said with a bit more authority. "If you went through all the trouble to become this beautiful woman, then act like a lady!" As she stood up, her boyfriend eagerly agreed with me, "I told her that." She just looked confused. I guess she'll get it all integrated in time or she won't. In either case, it's not for me to judge.

The point is, homosexuals, for lack of a better word (You know how I hate labels.) are people like everyone else, no more or less sinful than anyone else. We are not by default perverts or deviants or child molesters. We need love and acceptance and companionship and relationship, like everyone else. We just happen to have a proclivity to seek those things from people of the same sex as ourselves.

As I shared with you before, I don't fully understand why I spiritually, emotionally, and physically LOVE women. I have ascertained that it is partially genetic and partially of environmental influence. Does the molestation have something to do with it? Probably. My assumption at an early age of responsibility for my mother's well-being? Possibly. Hollis's violent behavior? Could be. Not being liked by the boys I liked in junior high school? Perhaps, although I liked girls way before junior high school. My birth sign, my rising sign, or because Venus was in conjunction with Mars at the moment of my conception—who knows? A combination of all the above? More than likely.

There are so many factors involved in what makes us who we are and why we do the things we do. The quest for understanding is all part of the journey. Of one thing I am certain: God knows exactly who I am and what I am and why I am. He tells us in Jeremiah 1:5, "Before you were formed in the womb, I knew you." I stand on David's prayer in Psalms 139:13, "For you created my inmost being; you knit me together in my mother's womb. I praise you because I am fearfully and wonderfully made; marvelous are your works. This, my soul knows very well. My frame was not hidden from you when I was made in the secret place. When I was woven together in the depths of the earth, your eyes saw my unformed body." So I guess when you think about it, we are all variants because we are each individually, "fearfully and wonderfully made." And some of us were made to love and share our lives with others of the same sex. Some of us were, created that way. Jesus even states in Matthew 19:12, "For some are eunuchs because they were born that way; others were made that way by men." I don't know how common it is for men to be born without testicles; I would speculate not common at all. So was Jesus speaking metaphorically?

Many of the Biblical references to homosexual behavior were directed to heterosexuals who were expressing deviant behavior. There are many practices and laws in The Bible that simply are not applicable in this day and age. And remember, the Old Testament was written for and about the Hebrews. Gentiles (a.k.a. Christians) don't come on the scene until the New Testament. I found an excellent essay online called "Homosexuality and the Bible" by Reverend Dr. Walter Wink. He references Biblical quotes pertaining to homosexuality and puts them in historical and sociological perspective.

One label I will claim: Child of God! My Father loves me, this I know, not only because the Bible tells me so, but because He has shown me in so many ways. He has delivered me time and again from my foolishness. He has rescued me from myself. He talks to me. In fact, He's the one who encouraged me to write this book and wouldn't let me rest until it was completed. He has spared my life, giving me time to grow, to know Him better, and to know His ways and His wants for me, for His glory. And so far, He hasn't indicated to me that He has a problem with me loving women.

Jesus even tells us in Luke 12:57, "Why don't you judge for yourselves what is right?" Like I said before, I'm not always the most obedient child of God, but I do strive to hear what He is telling me and to adhere to His words. I am not promiscuous; I am wiser than that now—Glory to God. But I do date women and pray that God will bless me with a good and godly wife someday. Oh, and on that subject, the Bible also tells us in Romans 13:1, "Everyone must submit himself to the governing authorities, for there is no authority except that which God has established. The authorities that exist, have been established by God. Consequently, he who rebels against the authority is rebelling against what God has instituted and those who do so will bring judgment on themselves." There are currently several countries in which same-sex marriage is legal, and praise the Lord, the Supreme Court has ruled that same-sex marriage is legal in all fifty of these United States!

Wouldn't it be good if Mary and Alice and the whole LGBT community felt welcome to get spiritual counsel and support from the Church, the body of Christ? Wouldn't our Heavenly Father want them to know and believe He is their Father, too, and that He loves them also? Wouldn't He want them to feel welcome to come to Him to pray for guidance? Perhaps we would all be better served by more sermons condemning hatred in all its insidious forms and allowing consenting adults to love each other without prejudice or persecution. Please understand, although I am calling Christians out, I am addressing all religious zealots who are using their religion to justify hate and judgment instead of walking in love.

PEACE

By the year 2000, I owned three rental properties in New York: The twenty-six unit in the South Bronx, a five unit rooming house in Bedford Park, and a six unit pain in the neck in Yonkers. After stressing me out for a year, my fifteen-year-old niece had moved back to Ohio with her parents. The disability insurance company was still harassing me. And, my relationship with Maria was approaching an inevitable re-defining.

During this time, I prayed and read my Bible daily and was beginning to assimilate it into my spirit. As the Lord spoke to me through his word, I began to get some revelations about my life. One of my first major realizations was how important it is to have peace. Although I lived in solitude, in serene country surroundings, my life was anything but peaceful. Even though being a landlord was lucrative, it was the most stressful occupation I ever had. I was on the job 24/7 and there was always some dilemma or other. My cell phone was the main contact number for my tenants and I literally would cringe whenever it rang. It was time to start selling some of the properties and lighten my load. Also, the disability insurance company had to go. They hounded and harassed me so, that instead of focusing on my abilities, I was more focused on my disability in order to justify the continuation of my benefits. After all, I was being paid to be disabled. They had offered to buy me out of my policy a few times but I would have been sacrificing millions of dollars in the long run.

I discussed it with my accountant who told me to suck it up and deal with the harassment. Detectives followed me all around New York, from the country to the city and back. After a while, it seemed a bit too blatant; it was probably some kind of psychological intimidation. The detectives would also lurk in the woods surrounding my house, waiting for me to play tennis or lift a load that seemed too heavy. I hired an attorney in an attempt to get them to offer more money or to just back off. We were able to attain all their documentation regarding my case, including the surveillance records.

The surveillance reports alone were as voluminous as three Manhattan phone books! They reported peering through my bedroom window; I suppose to see if I was performing any acrobatic sexual acts. I was required to go to my doctor every month for an update on my condition and then to go to their doctors for a rebuttal of the updates. The entire process became increasingly annoying. I even began to feel ripped off by my attorney due to all the billable hours of doing nothing. One of the insurance company specialists asked, "Why do you feel you can't return to work?"

I quickly answered, "Because, I'm in pain." Which, I was.

Afterwards, I thought about it. This was all like some waiting game to see who's going to wait out or fake out whom. I was led to write their specialist a letter, answering the question why I couldn't return to work at that time. In essence, I explained how all during my professional career as a physical therapist I never had an incident in which I harmed any of my patients, but in my current condition, I could no longer guarantee that. It was time to be rid of them, but I wanted the best payout possible. I think my letter did it. I was tired of being dis-abled. But everything that was involved for me to keep getting paid also prevented me from being healed.

At the beginning of 2000, I accepted their offer of a payout. I sacrificed well over two million dollars that I would have received if I had remained on disability until age sixty-five, but at what cost? I would have no peace of mind. Even days that I may have felt better or could have done more, I couldn't for fear of being seen. It wasn't prudent to allow myself to get better physically because that's not what I was being paid to do. You can't put a price on peace or your health; they are priceless. Because God has favored me with such a wonderful mind, body, and spirit, I want it all to be the best that it can be, the best that I can be. So, the insurance company and I happily (on both sides) parted ways. All things considered, I was blessed.

Maria and I met in 1985 at one of the nursing homes where I consulted. Maria, a chocolate brown, tall, beautiful and sophisticated woman was thirteen years my elder. At the time, she was dating the owner of the nursing home. I was attracted to her from the very beginning, however, she was seeing my employer and I was quite involved in a volatile relationship with Dana, so it was not our time. We undoubtedly shared a mutual admiration for one another, and she always had my back at work. During that time my practice in Brooklyn was growing, so shortly after my mother's death, I gave up some of my consulting positions in the Bronx. Maria and I lost touch.

One evening in 1991 I received a phone call. "Melanie, I don't know if you remember me?"

"Maria!" How excited I was to hear her sultry voice.

"Oh, wow, you do remember me." She sounded a bit thrown.

She came over that night, just to say hello. I knew right away that she was down on her luck and looking to hook up with someone with money. There was an ever so subtle hint of desperation in her eyes. Attraction and admiration may have had something to do with her reaching out to me, but I knew money was at the root. I didn't care. Most of my past relationships had been with "straight" women, and I knew, however it started, in the end, she would love me. That was usually the case. I proceeded to court Maria. Shortly afterwards, we became lovers, although lovemaking was not one of her greater interests. It had nothing to do with my gender. When we got together I was thirty-eight, and she was already postmenopausal. The fact that we didn't have a passionate sexual relationship was fine with me. After my relationship with Dana, I needed a respite from passion. Maria was broke financially, and I was broke emotionally and spiritually. I needed healing and not the sexual healing that Marvin Gaye sings about.

It's so interesting how this woman just called me out of the clear blue. We hadn't worked together for years and had never socialized together. Dana and I had broken up. Maria was in need and so was I. And, we each had what the other needed. God is so...good! He acts through people. He uses people like us to bless each other, to help each other through, to stand in the gap for one another, and to give an encouraging word and a guiding hand. The Lord works through us.

Maria and I became good friends and business partners. She was a real estate broker, but business was a bit slow for her when we first hooked up. She negotiated my first investment property deal in 1992, a five-family, turn of the century brownstone in Bedford Park, the Bronx. The prior owner was running an illegal rooming house in four of the apartments, and he lived in the fifth apartment with his family. He was making plenty of what looked like easy money. After I took over, I found it was not as easy as it looked. Maria helped me manage the property, all the properties, in fact.

The second property I purchased through her was the twenty-six unit I spoke about previously. In order to help her secure her future, I allowed her to buy into the property using the broker's commission that she earned from the sale of the property, about sixteen thousand dollars. She now owned six percent of the property.

I was very generous to Maria. We went on many trips: a safari in Tanzania and extended visits to Costa Rica, Panama, and South Africa, to name a few. We traveled well together and had many memorable experiences. I paid for most of our travel and entertainment expenses, in addition to helping her with her rent and other financial needs. I didn't mind. We had a mutually beneficial relationship, and although it may have been initiated for financial gain on her part, she became a true and loyal friend.

We were family. Her family became my family and mine became hers. I remember in the early years, though, her sister, who professed to be a Christian, asked Maria not to bring me to Thanksgiving dinner because she did not approve of our relationship. Maria told her if I was not welcome, then neither was she. I went to Thanksgiving dinner that year and every year afterwards for the next ten years. Her sister learned to make peace with our relationship and developed a genuine affection for me.

Again, people often treat you according to how you present yourself and what you accept from them. Maria was the closest I have ever come to having a wife. But on a much deeper level, she gave me the nurturing, support, and security that I lacked as a child. Her love was greatly instrumental in helping heal my wounds although I still had a long way to go. As our years together progressed, her nurturing support began to feel more maternal to me than marital. This posed a problem as I was still relatively young. Gradually, I began to miss physical intimacy and passion. I never cheated, we were loyal to each other. But as my desire for passion grew, I found myself looking at other women and wanting to be with them.

I knew our relationship needed to be redefined.

I started preparing her for the inevitable. During the latter years, I expressed my concerns to her regarding our lack of physical intimacy, although by that time, I didn't really want it with her, as I no longer regarded her sexually. Our relationship had become a cherished friendship. I bought her a brand new car for her birthday so she would have reliable transportation, which she needed in her business. I didn't want to hurt her or desert her, but I've always believed in being true to myself.

On New Year's Eve 2002, Maria and I had an argument, which seemed to be happening with an increasing frequency. On this particular night, she told me I was smothering her. How comically ironic when in fact, I was actually trying my best to ease out of the relationship. Well, that was my cue. "You won't have to worry about me smothering you anymore," I told her. I couldn't make a grand exit, because it was too late to drive upstate, but I knew our relationship was over.

The next day, I went home to mourn and inform my friends and family of our new status. While we remained friends and business partners, as far as I was concerned, we were no longer partners in love. Apparently, I didn't make it clear when I left that day or for days and months after. It was spring of 2003. I was in the Bahamas, at my recently built beach house, when Maria called and told me that our mutual friend Yolanda had expressed her condolences over the demise of our relationship. She acted as if she couldn't understand Yolanda's sympathy. The whole ordeal of breaking up with Maria caused me much grief, but she was acting as if it were no big thing. I said, "Yeah, Maria, it's something that should be mourned, after all we were together for ten years."

To my great surprise, she really didn't know what I was talking about. She hadn't even realized that the nature of our relationship had changed. Wow! That only demonstrated that it was a friendship and business partnership for many years. Maybe she just didn't want to know. No more free trips or paid rent; she was on her own. Our conversation remained civil as we resumed our discussion of the business at hand.

I had been in the Bahamas for three months, and just when I was reveling in my newfound freedom I met Samantha. Back then I tended to go from relationship to relationship. Anyway, when I returned to New York later that spring and informed Maria that I had met someone, she behaved scornfully and accused me of cheating her out of her six percent of the profits, demanding audits and such. She would call and threaten me with legal action, and she even went so far as to hire an attorney. I was devastated and deeply hurt because I had already given Maria at least five times her initial investment (what I had allowed her to invest) in the building. I was not going to suffer this harassment indefinitely, so I offered to buy her out for twenty-five thousand dollars, which was a fair estimate of what six percent of the building was worth. But Maria was determined to get much more. I decided to sell the building (again the peace of mind factor). She got her six percent, which was a little less than twenty-five thousand dollars, but she also had her legal fees to pay. She, therefore, gained less than she could have, had she accepted my initial offer.

It was ultimately a blessing because I sold before the collapse of the real estate market, and I made a sizable profit. Plus, I had peace. I tried to reestablish a friendship with Maria after the dust had settled, but she was having no part of it. Upon my initiation, we would speak briefly from time to time. Then a couple of years after our break-up I called her on her birthday. Two sentences into the conversation she began to express her bitterness again. I explained to her that having unforgiveness in your heart is like swallowing poison and hoping the other person will die. It's true. Just this week, I was angry with someone, and I had a hard time forgiving her. After much prayer, we made peace this morning. I felt fifty pounds lighter. Negative feelings are heavy; they weigh you down.

On a daily basis, almost all of us Christians mindlessly recite the Lord's Prayer. Even you unbelievers know it, right? Do you ever pay attention to this part: "forgive our trespasses as we forgive those who trespass against us"? We are asking God to treat us the way we treat others, forgiveness-wise, that is. This blew my mind when I actually realized what I was praying. In Matthew 6:14, right after Jesus tells us The Lord's Prayer, he says, "For if you forgive men when they sin against you, your heavenly Father will also forgive you. But if you do not forgive men their sins, your Father will not forgive you." I really do try to practice not being easily offended by others, and if I am, I do try to understand and forgive as soon as possible.

I still have love for Maria. I always will. I believe once you've truly loved someone, your love doesn't go away even though the nature of the relationship may need to be redefined. Maria helped me to heal, and for this, I will be eternally grateful to her. I do believe God brought us together to bless each other. I pray, one day, she will allow herself to feel the same.

COMPANIONS & CONTRACTORS

So yeah, the beach house in the Bahamas. Around 1990, one of my elderly patients asked me if I would be interested in buying her property in Exuma. She said she had observed how I like to vacation in the islands and thought I might be interested in a property she purchased many years ago. She recently had a stroke and had given up on her dream of building a home in Exuma. She offered to sell me the lot at cost, so I went to check it out. I had never heard of the island and didn't even realize it was in the Bahamas. Her lot was located a block away from a beautiful beach.

    I had always wanted a beachfront house after visiting the home of my good friend Captain Leroy Watson of Grand Cayman, who took pride in being the first Black Merchant Marine sea captain. Dana was from Grand Cayman, so I met Leroy during my first visit to her home in 1986. He was pedaling his bicycle down the Queens Highway, a narrow, poorly paved road, hardly regal, towards Dana's house. I sat on the porch watching this middle-aged man on a woman's bike struggle up the little rise, as they called it. Leroy was tall and thin with salt and pepper hair, a ruggedly handsome man with a ruddy complexion. He stopped and greeted me in his deep gruff voice, "Hey, how you doin'? Dana around?" She came out onto the porch of her family's small stone house, barely one step above a shack. Introductions were made and we all chatted for a while. He seemed to welcome the shade the porch provided after pedaling in the hot sun. He explained how his license had been suspended for driving while intoxicated. We soon became fast friends.

The Captain and I both drank Johnny Walker Black Scotch, so every night we would see who would be the last one standing. I could usually drink him under the table. My liver was much younger then. He was a very kind and generous man who made his home accessible to just about any female who asked. Grand Cayman became one of my favorite vacation spots. The Captain's house was on a beach that was rich with coral. I would lie on the beach all day, listening to my Walkman (predecessor to iPod), smoking herb, and drinking beer, after which I would go out snorkeling. There were all kinds of fish, like moray eels, hiding in coral, popping their heads out just to freak you out. There were lobster, conch, barracuda, and beautiful coral, all kinds, all colors. Grand Cayman is surrounded by coral reef, so the waters were abundantly blessed with sea life. Some of the most fascinating and memorable moments of my life were spent in those waters on that beach. Sometimes, the Captain and I would go out diving for conch. Actually, I did the diving because the Captain couldn't swim. He would man the boat, a seventeen-foot Boston Whaler, and get out his glass bottom box to spot the conch. Then I would skin dive to the floor of the crystal clear sea to retrieve them.

As the years went on and the Captain was well into his sixties, the smoking and drinking started to take their toll on him. He even gave up smoking when he began to manifest a throat problem, maybe cancer. When I visited him the following year, he had resumed smoking.

"Captain, I thought you gave up smoking?" I asked with great concern.

He held up his pack of Viceroy cigarettes and hoarsely

Me & the Captain

uttered, "These are my companions. I am out at sea for months at a time, and my scotch and cigarettes are my faithful companions."

I didn't realize the magnitude of what he was saying until much later in life. When we think of our companions, we usually think of people, our friends or associates. Webster's Dictionary defines *companion* as "an intimate friend or associate; comrade; one who is closely connected with something similar." In truth and reality, though, as so perspicaciously observed by my good friend The Captain, companions can come in many forms.

Sadly, many of us don't have good mortal companions or any mortal companion at all. It seems, in fact, we are moving away from human companionship more and more to attachments with things. How many of us walk around, smart phone in hand, communicating with friends, associates, business affiliates, et cetera? We can reach out and touch just about anyone in the world, even see them through our smart phones or computers. We can engage in games with strangers from around the world, but we have no intimacy (in to me see) with them. The smart phone, the computer, they are the true companions. There have been several studies done on internet addiction. In addition to playing games, which is highly addictive, people have sex online; they can gamble, shop, chat, or even date, all from the comfort of their homes.

Funny thing about the dating websites, you spend more time cruising the site than actually interacting with anyone. So again, the computer becomes the companion. One doesn't have to physically interact with another for almost anything. We are truly entering the age of virtuality.

Folks would rather text you than actually talk to you. I'm sure you've experienced this. You can call someone and leave message after message and get no response. But text them once, and they respond immediately, especially the younger folks. Companionship? Leroy had it right years ago, even before the internet. How many of us sit in front of our televisions for hours, clinging to our remotes? Just recently, I met my good friend, Linda, for a girl's weekend away. We went out to dinner and had a few drinks. The next morning, Linda was teasing me about my actions the previous night. "Wow," she said laughing. "You got in your bed, turned on the TV, and then fell asleep. I asked you to turn it off, and you scolded me for waking you up. Then you pulled the remote out from under your covers, turned off the TV, and put the remote back under the covers with you."

All I could say was, "my companion." Have you ever seen an alcoholic come out of the liquor store lovingly clutching on to his or her bottle, or overeaters whose eyes go all aglow when they get their hands on that cheesecake? Companion!

To some, even pain can become a companion. I remember a couple of years ago when I was in absolute agony with cervical (neck) pain radiating down my arm. I consulted a local orthopedist who prescribed Oxycodone for me. One day, I had to drive to the city for a funeral. My pain was so severe, I took an Oxycodone. The pain persisted throughout the funeral. I stopped at a friend's on the way home, and she gave me 800 mg. of Motrin. While at her house I drank a bottle of wine and drove home stone cold sober as the pain completely overruled the medication. That episode of acute cervical pain lasted a month, during which time I hardly slept. Knowing well my proclivity to narcotics, I didn't want to open Pandora's box, so I would only take the Oxycodone at night. Even though the pain was so great, I wasn't getting high. In fact, I was barely getting relief. Eventually the pain subsided.

A year later my neck flared up again, this time with headaches. I had some Oxycodone left from the previous year, so I began taking one in the evenings and taking Tylenol during the day. Well, that first Oxycodone did have an intoxicating effect on me. In fact, it felt so good (the closest I had felt to a heroin high since I was fourteen) that I started craving a cigarette, even though I had quit smoking years prior. It did help to relieve the pain, but in the morning the pain would recur. Again, I took Tylenol during the day and saved the Oxycodone for the night.

I began to look anticipatorily for the pain and the subsequent medication. The pain and the medication, that sounds familiar, doesn't it? Writing this book has been revelational to me! Fortunately, the pain only lasted a few weeks that time, and thankfully, I didn't welcome either pain or medication as a companion. Even when we suspect or know that our companions are bad for us, are killing us, often we just won't let them go. It occurs to me our companions frequently become our addictions.

Like the Captain, my friend Beverli from Phoenix House,

the one who took me to my first lesbian bar, also chose cigarettes as one of her companions. We lost touch for many years, but when I moved upstate, I happened to see her name on the masthead of a magazine, as the editor and publisher. We reconnected. She had one of her lungs removed in the early 1990s because of lung cancer, yet she continued to smoke. Around 2003, she became ill again and was informed that she would have to have a piece of her remaining lung removed because the cancer had recurred. She survived the surgery, but she was dependent on a portable oxygen tank in order to breathe. Even that didn't end her primary relationship with her companion. As comedian Bernie Mac used to ask, "Who you with?"

I have had many companions in my life, some human and some not, some edifying and some not. Cigarettes were my companions from the time I was about twelve until I was about forty-two years old. I remember my last cigarette. My niece Candice was living with me at the time, and she was smoking at the age of fourteen. I had felt conflicted about smoking for many years. In my twenties I even quit for a while, but got pulled back in. The time to quit had come, plus I wanted to be a good example for my niece. I wanted to show her that smoking was not a good thing and that one did not have to do it. That provided the extra incentive I needed to stop. Remember, like I said before, sometimes we don't have enough self love to do the right thing for ourselves. Sometimes, it's the love for another that inspires us to take positive action. I proclaimed to Candice and myself that I had smoked my last cigarette, bravely marching outside to the trash can at the end of the property with my not yet empty pack.

We spent the day in the city, and as we were driving home, all I could think about were my cigarettes in the trash. When we arrived home, I sent Candice to bed and sat in my bedroom, thinking about those cigarettes. I finally broke down, got a flashlight, and sneaked out of the house, where, flashlight in mouth, I dug through the trash for those two, dear cigarettes. When I finally found them, I rushed back to my bedroom, closed the door, and opened the windows wide. Ah, a cigarette never tasted so good. But after they were gone, I had to laugh at myself. How pitiful are you? That ended my companionship with cigarettes.

I don't ever want to take my blessings for granted. I'm still a work in progress, and I am not perfect. Neither by the way, is anyone else. The battle, indeed, begins in the mind. In First Corinthians 6:12, Paul states "Everything is permissible for me, but not everything is edifying. Everything is permissible for me, but I will not be mastered by anything."

We all have our struggles, our thorns in the flesh. That is what the journey is about: to grow, to grow in the Spirit and overcome our flesh. So, choose your companions well. As Mahatma Gandhi once said, "Your beliefs become your thoughts, your thoughts become your words, your words become your actions, your actions become your values, your values become your destiny."

I will always remember The Captain for the great revelation on companionship. Ironically, he died at sea, in his own backyard, that wondrous playground with all the coral and fish. He was tying up his boat after a leisurely ride and must have had a heart attack or something. They discovered his body in the water. Anchors aweigh, Captain!

Anyway, back to the beach house in the Bahamas. When I first visited Exuma in 1990, I stayed in a hotel called Peace & Plenty, right in the middle of Georgetown. I was immediately impressed by the apparent affluence of the inhabitants of the island. Everyone was driving around in Acura Legends or better, blasting music and having a good time. It wasn't until many years later that I discovered the affluence was generated by drug trafficking. I was a bit spaced out myself at the time, so I guess I just didn't notice. Exuma is actually known as the Exuma Cays, a chain of about 360 small islands and cays. Greater Exuma, thirty-seven miles long, is the largest of the islands and is joined to Little Exuma by a partially wooden, single lane bridge. The drug trade was ended long ago and Exuma has since become quite the playground for the rich and famous.

Georgetown is the capital of the island. Back then, Exuma was a relatively undiscovered treasure, with its many beautiful, pristine beaches. Elizabeth Harbor, which is right in the center of Georgetown, was a haven for Captain Kidd long ago. At present, it is a popular winter home for many yachters and boaters from abroad.

I rented a car and explored on my own for a few days to get the feel of the island. I had never seen such crystal clear blue waters throughout my travels in the Caribbean. I visited one of the realtors in town to have them show me Mrs. Bailey's (my patient) property, in addition to any beachfront properties they had available. The agent, Hugo, was an attractive Bahamian man around my age. He took me to Little Exuma first to see Mrs. Bailey's property, a small lot about a block away from a fantastic beach. There were a couple of houses in the area, but for the most part, it was pretty uninhabited. Perfect, this was a go.

Hugo took me all around Greater and Little Exuma. There were a lot of beachfront properties available. It seemed the whole island was for sale. I finally decided on a lot right on the beach, close to Mrs. Bailey's property. There were five contiguous lots available (if I knew then what I know now). Hugo recommended what he believed to be the better of the lots, and so I proceeded to buy beachfront property in the Bahamas. Initially, I wanted beachfront property in Grand Cayman, and I did investigate the possibilities. But I couldn't wrap my mind around the idea of losing twenty percent of my money's value as soon as I stepped off the plane in Grand Cayman. That was too expensive a lifestyle for me, so the Bahamas it was.

I spent ten days or so in Exuma that first trip and met some of the locals. The more elite of the drug traffickers would meet at my hotel in the evenings for champagne, dancing, and merriment—my kind of town. Thank goodness I was ignorant about the nature of their wealth, or I might have made a good cocaine connection and fallen right back into that whole scene. But My Father was looking out for me. I did a little scuba diving, and one of the biggest traffickers took me out on his boat to go snorkeling. I even had sex with Hugo while I was there. Don't know what got into to me then. The sea, the sun, something about the islands tends to get one's libido all stirred up. Well, the sexual encounter with Hugo took all of five minutes and days of worry when I got home. We foolishly had unsafe sex, something I regretted the moment the brief, unsatisfying act was over. When I got home and didn't get my period on time, there was the fear of pregnancy, along with the additional possibility of HIV infection. I did finally get my period, and I got my very first HIV test, anonymously, at the board of health. Thankfully, it was negative. That was the last time I had sex with a man. I was scared straight, or to be more accurate, scared gay.

I kept a photograph of my beach above my desk at the HMO. It was my motivation to continue to work hard and make lots of money. Finally in 1999, I began planning to build the house. I kind of knew what I had in mind, something like the Captain's, with the bedrooms on the ocean side of the house so the waves could soothe me to sleep each night. I also knew that I wanted my king size bed to face the ocean, so when I woke up and looked over my big toe, the first thing I would see every morning would be the ocean. I began to draw up plans as I envisioned the house. Not being an architect, the plans were rough, but I drew my bedroom just about to scale. I planned to make it a two-family house, so when I had guests they would have their own separate space. I need time for myself, and I generally don't like sharing bathrooms. So, by the beginning of 2000, it was time to hire an architect and a contractor.

I had flown to Exuma from Grand Cayman, which was to be my last visit with the Captain. There were only a few houses on the beach at the time, including the little, pink cottage I was renting. That first night, I sat in the bed, windows open, reading a book and listening to the ocean waves. Ah! This was the life, the sea breeze, waves lapping upon the shore, the endless stars, simply amazing. But then I started itching, initially, just around my ankles and lower legs. It got progressively and rapidly worse as it spread to my arms and torso. Thinking perhaps the sheets were dirty, I changed the linen, took a shower and got back into bed for a long, sleepless night. The next morning, I met with Richie, a contractor. I was scratching my body like some dope fiend. (Itchiness is one of the side effects of heroin use.) Richie was personable and young. He hadn't yet ever built an entire house, but he had finished houses that other contractors had botched or abandoned. Throughout our meeting, I apologized for my incessant scratching. Anyway, he seemed cool, his price was right, he was available immediately, and so it was a go.

I didn't remain in Exuma long. The itching persisted. Was it the lobster dinner the Captain and I had the night before I left Grand Cayman? Was I becoming allergic to shellfish? Back in New York, the itching continued to worsen. I broke out in hives and contacted my doctor. He said he would phone in a prescription for steroids.

"What are you talking about, man? You want me to take

steroids for an itch? Come on." I declined his offer. A few days later, after applying home remedies of ammonia and bleach and whatever other madness Maria came up with in the middle of the night so I would let her sleep, I humbly called my doctor again.

"Could you phone in that prescription for the steroids, please?"

All that summer, I avoided shellfish, believing I had developed some kind of allergy. In the fall, it was time to go back to Exuma to check on the progress. I stayed with a couple who owned a guesthouse on another beautiful beach about ten minutes from my house. Saundra (the owner's girlfriend) and I were sitting outside having a drink when the itchiness returned. When I mentioned this to her, she replied, "Ah narseeums."

"What?"

"Narseeums."

"What are you saying, narseeums?" She was from New Zealand, so I thought I was losing something in the translation.

"NO-SEE-UMS, 'cause you can't see them—sandflies. They come out at dusk."

I grabbed my drink and flew into my room. The next evening, Derek (the owner) summoned me to receive a phone call. The phone was outside by the bar. I stuck my head out the door, "Is it safe?"

Derek burst out laughing, "Mon...dey got you traumatized, mon." And so they had.

Anyone who has built a house anywhere in the world or had to have any construction or contracting work done, knows what a potential nightmare it can be. Having work done in another country is additionally frustrating as one is not there to monitor the work. Typically, contractors will commit themselves to more than one project at a time. When they know you are coming down, they'll work on your project. When you leave, they pack up the crew and proceed to their other projects. I have heard many horror stories of unfinished houses and court battles. Almost no one goes unscathed. I was blessed.

Richie was making good progress with the house, and we came to an amazing meeting of the minds. Where the plans fell short, I would describe to him what I envisioned and he worked it out, beautifully. He is an excellent problem solver, a talented carpenter and best of all, a man of integrity, truly a blessing from God. My house was completed in a little over a year, at the end of 2002, record time for the Bahamas and probably most places around the world. It's not a mansion, but it is a very well built, comfortable home.

SAMANTHA

I met Samantha, a Bahamian woman, in Exuma. We were introduced by Freddie, one of the guys who used to hang around in town all day, drinking. Kind, educated and perceptive, Freddie wasn't a bad man. I don't know his story, but I'd guess he made some poor choices along the way. He kept telling me he had someone that he wanted me to meet. "I know what you like," he'd say. So, one day, while grocery shopping Freddie dragged me across the street to meet a woman who was selling conch (not a euphemism for anything; she was collecting money for the conch salad vendor). There were a couple of other Bahamian women next to her when Freddie introduced us. He was cool and didn't intimate anything. Samantha was a massage therapist and that's how he introduced her. I could feel the other women looking on mockingly, dying to talk about "dat sissy" as soon as I left. I chatted with Samantha for a bit and got her business card to schedule a massage.

I do love massages.

A few days later, on Good Friday, I went to Samantha's studio for a massage. I could see right away that she was a bit insecure and nervous. She was a damn good massage therapist, though. She told me that she lived right down the beach from me in the little yellow cottage. I remembered seeing her a couple of times, once driving by my house and once on the beach. I assumed she was some depressed Bahamian housewife, living in the area with her womanizing husband. One night, before I was introduced to Samantha, Derek and Saundra had come to my house for dinner. I later learned that Derek, without my knowledge, had gone to Samantha's and invited her over, telling her he thought we should meet. She declined because the invitation had not come from me. I never knew that she was living just two houses away, but what's to be will be.

After my massage, I invited Samantha to come over the next night for cocktails. She walked along the beach to my house, and when she reached the top of the stairs, I met her with open arms. She later told me how much that moved her. We drank some champagne and talked. She was forty-five years old and had a grown son in the States. The age was right, and I liked that she was a mother; mothers tend to be more loving, or so we would think. Anyway, I was open about my sexuality and my newly established freedom. She told me she and her husband were separated. We danced, I believe at her initiation, and after a while I was tired and ready for bed. She told me that her cousin was staying at her cottage and there was only one bed. I offered her my couch, but she said she would much rather sleep with me. And so we began. Samantha had never been with a woman before.

Samantha smelled sweet all over and was soft to the touch. She had big, tender thighs and a beautiful behind, while above the waist she was almost petite. Her voice was silky and touched my heart. Our bodies fit well together and lying next to her was heavenly. I found her to be almost magical. We kissed that night and held each other. It was good. No unsafe sex until we had HIV tests. I wasn't going through the traumatic what-ifs ever again if I could help it.

I only had a few weeks left in Exuma before returning to New York. We spent a lot of time together, so much for my celebrated freedom and plans to be a player for a little while. Before I left Exuma, I was led to invite Samantha to live in my house and be the caretaker. She looked up to heaven as if her prayers had been answered. I suspected she was way behind in her rent at the cottage. My only stipulation was that she could not entertain anyone in my house. I was just trying to give her the opportunity to save some money and get herself together. You see, although she was in relationship with The Lord, she wasn't at a great place in her life at that time.

I left for New York, and although it had only been a few weeks, for all intents and purposes, I was already, emotionally, in a committed relationship. Crazy, right? I mean, I didn't really know this woman who lived a thousand miles away. I just came out of a ten-year relationship and was looking forward to dating, or so I thought.

Samantha came to New York a few months later to visit for a month. A few months after her visit, I returned to Exuma. That's when she told me she had a boyfriend. Wow! Were they sleeping in my bed? I had stopped drinking a couple of months earlier, considering Sam didn't particularly like when I drank. I was so proud of myself. After she dropped this bomb on me, I not only wanted a drink, but even more so, I craved a cigarette. I did have some drinks and a cigarette the following day and for a couple of days after that. One day, while buying some cognac, I was tempted to buy a pack of cigarettes. I knew if I did that, my old companion would be back for good, so I didn't and haven't had a cigarette since.

Well, we got past the boyfriend thing, but long story short, there was always one thing or another, and there was always hurt. During our second year "together," Samantha got a job with a major hotel chain and transferred to New York. I provided her with monetary support and an apartment in one of my properties, rent free, of course. Now understand, contrary to how it seems, I'm no fool. Despite my propensity to be the caretaker, I am also very business oriented and believe in reciprocation. But with Samantha, hurt after hurt, disappointment after disappointment, I still hung in there.

It was mind-boggling. I would cry to my friends about how she wronged me again and again. I know they were sick of hearing about it after a while, because I was surely sick of talking about it. Little tidbit of information: folks don't really want to hear about your heartache and victimization. Your friends will tolerate it for a while and give you advice, but it soon becomes tiresome. Those who can identify with you, those who are experiencing heartache of their own, will listen to your blues only as they anxiously await their turn to share their story with you. Anyway, the years that I spent *with* Samantha, those seven years between 2003-2010, were to be a time of great revelation for me.

The Bible tells us in Proverbs 18:24, "A man of many companions may come to ruin, but there is a friend who sticks closer than a brother." I assume the friend is Jesus. I am very blessed to say that Jesus is now one of my companions. I am learning more and more everyday that He is the best companion I will ever have. I never thought I would believe that. I remember Samantha told me something similar when we first got together. She said that God was the only person she really needed in her life and that she wasn't into relationships, per se. I remember thinking, "She's so full of it." That was twelve years ago. Now, I understand.

Don't get me wrong, I still want a human companion, a life partner, someone I can hold and kiss: with whom I can share time, space and energy, someone I can truly love who will truly love me in return. The difference is that now, I don't desperately need that someone. If I had to, I could live without her/him because I have discovered that I am already deeply loved by my Heavenly Father. He has proven

His love to me time and again. I can't help but know it. God has blessed me beyond belief and has given me the time to grow up, to know Him, the time to grow in my love for Him, and the ability to love myself. And I now know that I am worthy of love. I have been blessed with family and friends with whom I can share my love and blessed with the willingness to feel and show love and compassion to whomever. So, thanks to God, now, I can walk in love. But Father, I think I would still really like to get married some day, okay?

It's so ironic. When Samantha and I first got together, I would feel very threatened by her relationship with God because I thought He would eventually take her away from me. When she turned on Christian TV programs, I was afraid they would start speaking against same-sex relationships as they often do, and this was already a conflict for Samantha, a huge conflict. The Bible tells us, "a double minded man is unstable in all his ways," and that was an understatement in this circumstance. I was in relationship with the Lord at the time but not as deeply as I am now. Nowadays, I watch Christian TV programs every morning, can't start my day without the Word. And the reality was, I never had Samantha to begin with.

First of all, she was married, although she had been separated from her husband for years. As we were becoming intimate, she expressed to me that she and her husband preferred to stay married because then they had an excuse for their inability to commit to anyone else. Maya Angelou very wisely once said, "When someone tells you who they are, believe them!" Samantha clearly told me she was unavailable, on so many levels, but I refused to hear and believe her. Plus, in all fairness to myself, she gave me mixed messages all the time.

I was like Pavlov's dog, classically conditioned. She would make herself available, mostly when she needed me and be unavailable when she didn't. Our sweet times together were very sweet and special but inconsistent. If memory serves me correctly, according to Pavlov, conditioning lasts longest when the reward is given inconsistently. When the treat is not supplied each time the bell rings but instead on an inconsistent basis, it is more difficult for the animal to become de-conditioned. He will keep looking for that reward each time the bell rings, believing in the possibility that this time, he would receive the reward. And so it was with Samantha and me. For seven long years, I tried to make her love me the way I thought I deserved to be loved. I tried to force her into the relationship that I thought we should have. And I mean I really tried, so hard that I almost had a complete breakdown.

The turning point came in 2009 when I finally fled to the nearest psychotherapist's office. I was depressed and frustrated and feeling so alone. After six years of what was in reality a non-relationship with Samantha, I had to accept two truths: I was being willful, foolish, and self-destructive, and the relationship I longed for was not the one I was in. I won't get into the gory details; suffice it to say that Samantha had issues too. Yet I could not get her out of my mind and heart. I would think of the mornings after we made love, how she would lie on top of me, and we would both drift back off to sleep. How our bodies seemed to fit so well together, her thighs almost as soft as her voice, and both would make me just melt. But those were moments sparsely dispersed over way too long a period of time. And it seemed our only cohesive moments were in bed.

Whenever I told her of my unfulfilled needs and desires, she would say that I needed to love her unconditionally, which I finally understood that she meant, "Don't make any demands on me, 'cause I don't want any responsibility in the relationship." I did love her unconditionally, and on many levels, she loved me too. After trying to fully understand what was wrong with those dynamics, why the words "I love you" didn't somehow accommodate the situation, it occurred to me that although I loved Samantha unconditionally, the very nature of relationships is conditional. Webster's dictionary includes as one of its definitions of relationship "the mutual exchange between two people or groups who have dealings with one another." When you are in a relationship with another, there are expectations to be met, implied or otherwise. There is an agreed upon reciprocity.

My friend Linda and I would talk on the phone for hours analyzing our failed relationships and psychoanalyzing our tainted lovers, who repeatedly professed their love for us, as they continued to break our hearts. Linda commented during one of our sessions, "There ought to be a law. They say they love you, but they should be made to spell it L-U-V, not L-O-V-E, so you know the difference." We laughed, but the next day I started looking for help. I couldn't shake the depression.

I called a therapist listed in my health insurance guide. The office looked like a clinic. The receptionist directed me upstairs to an empty room to wait for the therapist. I had never been to therapy before, so I didn't quite know what to expect. I just knew I needed to talk to someone to find out why I was feeling so down and why I had endured Samantha's emotional abuse for so long when even a blind man could see it was futile from the very beginning. Anyway, the therapist finally came, with a briefcase stuffed with papers. He ushered me into his office, sat behind a desk, pulled out some papers and proceeded to ask me questions—questions regarding my insurance and general information for billing purposes.

I sat there next to a box of tissues, fighting back the tears, answering his endless questions, anxiously awaiting to just get to it, the therapy part that is. A few tears did make their way down my cheeks. What the hell, just fix me, man! Next question, "Who is your emergency contact?"

"Emergency contact?" I burst into tears and could not stop sobbing. My mind searched desperately, hopelessly. *Emergency contact.* I continued to cry. Finally, I composed myself enough to mumble out my aunt's name and contact information. *How pathetic*, I thought. *You have to use your aunt as your emergency contact. You have no one.* I cried and cried. Finally, he asked me why I was there. All I could say was, "I can't stop crying." By that time, our therapy session was over, and he scheduled another appointment.

Big help, eh? But surprisingly, it was a big help. When I got home I thought about what had happened, especially when he asked for an emergency contact. For the first time, I became acutely, painfully aware that I really was ALONE. I had no one of my own: no mother, no brother, no lover, no child. No one! All throughout the endless losses, I always had someone. When Mommy died, I had Mama, my brother and my girlfriend. When Cliff and Mama died, I had Maria. When I lost my job, and when I lost my ability to have children, Maria was also there. When Maria and I separated, Samantha and I got together immediately afterward. But Samantha and I were not to have the relationship that Maria and I had. I was attempting to fill a vacuum.

For years, it boggled my mind that I remained with Samantha for so long when it was obviously so wrong. I still can't fathom completely what went on between us. My comprehension of our relationship comes in bits and pieces. For instance, aside from my willfulness and defiance, I finally realized that I was trying to resume my relationship with Maria, but with Samantha and the additional benefit of sex. It was the classic 80/20 rule. It goes like this: No one can give you one hundred percent of what you're looking for in a relationship. If you get eighty percent, you're doing exceptionally well, but sometimes we focus more on what we don't have than what we do have. Our perception can become so distorted that we take for granted the eighty percent that we have and focus so intensely on the twenty percent we are not getting in the relationship that it appears larger and more important than the eighty percent that we have. Subsequently, we leave the eighty percent to find the twenty percent.

But my relationship with Samantha was not for naught. Just as I believe God brought Maria and me together to help one another, the same holds true for Samantha and me. Only I think she needed the nurturing this time, and I needed to become painfully aware of some of my frailties, shortcomings, and unresolved issues. This had been yet another growth and learning opportunity along the journey. Now when I look at it, it's really quite simple and quite typical why I continued to relentlessly pursue a relationship with Samantha. I didn't want to be alone. The longer I stayed, the more of an investment I made. Being a businesswoman, innately willful and goal oriented, was the perfect set-up for me to stay in the relationship. But it was just that, a set up, and there was even more to be learned.

Samantha told me on more than one occasion that I was prideful, and so I was. I was also willful, emotionally needy, occasionally, a bit too hard on myself, and worst of all haughty eyed. Haughtiness is when one overestimates one's own abilities and underestimates another's. Haughty eyes have had me over extend myself for others on many occasions. Note, I said OVER extend. It's one thing to lend a helping hand, quite another to assume responsibility for another person's life altogether. All these things I learned about myself while in relationship with Samantha. All these things prolonged my relationship with Samantha. But I also learned how loving and kind and forgiving I am.

While I was writing this book, I referred back to my journals a lot. At one point, I named them the Samantha Chronicles because for seven years it was mostly all about Sam. After skimming through just some of it, I was sick of myself. Whew! It was embarrassing. What was wrong with me? I could only shake my head in reproach. But there were a lot of lessons to learn during that time, a lot of growing to do.

The day we finally came to an end was ugly. Samantha was selfish and inconsiderate, and I drank in response. It was early July of 2010, and Samantha and I had been off and on for years. It was like we just couldn't let each other go, no matter how bad it got. That day, July 7th, when I walked out of her door, I knew this had to be the last time. We couldn't be friends with benefits or spend a casual night together—all the ways we tried to have each other while pretending to be free of each other just didn't work. It always ended in pain, mostly mine. Anyway, I continued on with my life, dating, doing family things, and pursuing my walk with God. One day, He revealed this to me: "You have abandonment issues and Samantha has commitment issues, that's a match made in Hell!" But still, I thought about her, forgave her, and missed her. I began to pray to God to free me from my obsession with Samantha. I didn't want to think about her, didn't want to love her; I just wanted to be free of her. It was time to get off this not-so-merry-go-round.

The very first morning I asked God to free me, He directed me to Psalm 118: "Give thanks to the Lord for He is good, His love endures forever... In my anguish I cried out to the Lord and He set me free and in a large space. The Lord is with me, I will not be afraid. What can man do to me? The Lord is with me; He is my helper. I will look in triumph on my enemies. It is better to take refuge in the Lord than to trust in man. It is better to take refuge in the Lord than to trust in princes... The Lord is my strength and my song, he has become my salvation... This is the day the Lord has made; let us rejoice and be glad in it." I have abbreviated the psalm, but it is worth reading in its entirety.

Now like I said, I try to read my Bible everyday. Often when the Bible is new to us, we tend to just open it up randomly to see what the "Word" has for us, like magic. As I have been reading the Bible for many years, I seldom continue that practice. However, more often than not, I find that God usually gives me a word appropriate to my needs. I read that psalm over and over that day, feeling so close to Him. He repeatedly lets me know that He hears me. He sees me. That morning, no lie, I was freed. He did set me free and in a large space. I realized it was not Samantha from whom I needed liberation; it was from myself. I realized how blessed I was, and how much time, how many tears and years I had wasted because I lingered too long somewhere I should have left years before.

It had nothing to do with Samantha, or very little. I took myself through those changes by refusing to acknowledge what I knew in my heart. Don't complain about what you permit! From that day, my perception of Samantha, of relationships, of life, totally changed. Since that day, I begin each morning by saying, "This is the day the Lord has made. I will rejoice and be glad in it. Thank you, Father, for another day. Let me be a blessing today." I am thankful for every day now. And I will not shed unnecessary tears.

We waste so much time and energy as if we were to live forever. I have become acutely aware that I have lived more days on this earth than I have left to live. I want my remaining days to be as joyful and fruitful as humanly possible. I will let no one steal my joy, and I certainly am not going to throw it away. Sometimes I wonder if we don't get involved in relationships as diversions, preoccupations, if you will: another way to avoid ourselves, perhaps? Yes, we all want and need love and companionship. God wants us to be in relationship (the right relationship). He tells us, "two are better than one." But do we occasionally get involved in a relationship just to *have* someone or stay too long, even when we recognize that ultimately, it's not going to be fruitful, or it has outlived its purpose?

They say, "Some people are in our lives for a reason, some for a season." I've heard the analogy of a rocket ship used to describe some relationships. Sometimes people are like rocket boosters in our lives. The rocket boosters are attached to the rocket ship to aid in its ascension. However, at some point they have to detach, or they will only result in bringing the rocket back down. They become unnecessary weight and outlive their purpose. You've got to accept when it's time to let go.

I learned just how willful I can be. It's going to be *my* way, you'll see. Like the song from Dream Girls, "I'm stayin', I'm stayin', and YOU, YOU, YOU-you're gonna love me!" Wow! Maya was so right regarding this subject. "When someone tells you who they are, believe them." God does talk to us and provide us with what we need as we need it-if we have ears to hear and eyes to see. The only person I try to change these days is myself.

On September 1st of that year (2010) I got a call from Samantha's good friend. Samantha had been in the hospital for a few days. It was serious. She implored me to call, and although I was extremely reluctant to go down that road again—Sam often got "ill" after we broke up—I did. It was very serious and her family hadn't arrived in New York yet, so I went to the hospital. She had tubes down her throat and was so frail. Once again, my heart just welled up with love and a sense of protectiveness. I attended to her needs, rubbed her down with lotion, and tried to make her as comfortable and secure as possible. She was in the hospital for weeks, enduring a couple of surgeries and some near death moments, during which time I visited regularly. I loved her and had no reservations about showing it, 'cause it was different. I didn't want anything in return, not even her love. I didn't want a relationship or companionship or even friendship. I just loved her and tended to her needs. And when she was better and well taken care of, I could walk away, without any expectations. So, she finally got the unconditional love that she wanted from me, and I finally learned what unconditional love really is. We had come full circle.

Samantha and I still have love for each other, and now, we are in a relationship we can both accept, being friends and loving each other from afar.

THE HEALING CONTINUES

I didn't address my other "issue of blood," the hepatitis C, for many years after my diagnosis. I didn't realize the severity of the disease or that it even was a disease. It wasn't until 1999, a few years after learning of my hepatitis, that I discovered how deadly it truly was. My sister and her second husband, Tommy, were visiting me. Years earlier, Tommy had been diagnosed with hepatitis C. I was aware that my sister was very involved in helping him manage his condition, but that was the extent of my interest. His visit was my wake up call. He was thin and grey and knock, knock, knockin' on heaven's door. It was frightening. Is that what hepatitis C can do to you?

After their visit, I began to research hepatitis C and discovered it was an infectious disease of the liver. It is transmitted via blood-to-blood interaction as associated with transfusions, poorly sterilized medical equipment, or intravenous drug use. About eighty percent of those exposed to the virus develop chronic infections although they may remain asymptomatic for decades. About two percent of the U.S. population is infected with the virus, and annual deaths from infection range from 8,000 to 10,000. It can result in scarring of the liver, which could lead to cirrhosis of the liver, liver cancer, and quite possibly, a liver transplant. Drinking alcohol or taking medications that stress the liver are not recommended for persons with hepatitis C.

Well, as I was still at the beginning of my emotional/spiritual healing process, I was drinking alcohol indiscriminately. I was not ready to deal with the disease or stop drinking, and so I did neither.

By 2005 the time had finally come for me to address the matter of my disease. For the prior six years, I had been consuming alcohol on a regular basis and waking each morning with fear, guilt, and self-condemnation. We are responsible for what we know, and knowing how potentially deadly this disease could be and how I was only compounding the problem, creating an even more life-threatening scenario by drinking, then whatever the consequences, that's on me, yes? How could I even pray to God to heal me of this when I was guilty of doing things that could only exacerbate my condition? For six years, the guilt and condemnation haunted me. I thought of my friend Beverli and how critical I had been of her because she continued to smoke after having one lung and part of another removed. Yet wasn't I behaving just as foolishly? Wasn't I just as weak willed? What was wrong with me? Didn't I have enough self-love or will to live, to stop drinking, and deal with the problem? Was I taking my health and all my other many, many blessings for granted, tempting God? Day after day I woke with these questions and convictions. Night after night I continued to drink.

Wow! Ignorance is bliss, for a while, at least. Yes, there were some moments of sanity and self-control. In 2002, I stopped drinking for a couple of months. Then Maria and I went to South Africa where they were serving wine with breakfast, lunch and dinner. I lasted a few days, but after all, I was on vacation. I gave up alcohol again in 2004 for a couple of months until Samantha stressed me out, and I jumped right back off that wagon. There was always something—the buildings, the tenants, leaks, floods, heartaches, parties—always something. Justification could always be found. Finally, I was like, hey, if you're going to drink, it's because you want to drink, and if you are allowing yourself to do it, then don't feel guilty about it. We had a saying in Phoenix House "Guilt Kills," and so it does.

A few years before I sought treatment, I shared my diagnosis with my primary physician, who had been unaware of my hepatitis C. I started becoming concerned about my liver and wanted to monitor its condition to assuage my conscience, as it were. He asked me how I got hepatitis, and I told him I had no idea, unless I'd been exposed to it during my medical career. Even though physical therapists did not work with hypodermic needles, that excuse was as good as any. After all, it really wasn't any of his business that I was a heroin addict when I was thirteen. That was then, this is now. It didn't matter how I contracted it. The reality is I got it, so let's deal with it.

Since I didn't have the telltale track mark scars that so many ex-drug addicts have, no one needed to know, right? We began monitoring my liver enzymes to determine my liver function, and we did viral load counts to see if the hepatitis was progressing. Test after test, my doctor would call with the report. Each time, he would sound a bit more concerned and a bit more reprimanding. "Your viral load is 400,000. Your viral load is 600,000. Your viral load is 800,000!" Initially, all I heard was blah, blah, blah. Then one day following the most recent blood test, he called, and this time when he reported the hundreds of thousands of my viral load, it registered. "How many hundreds of thousands? Is that bad?" On top of that, my stools were turning white. I looked that up on the internet too, and learned it was a symptom of liver disease. It was time to face the music and dance. I made an appointment for a consultation to get a referral for treatment.

Why now, after all these years of denial? I think during that time was when I began to acknowledge my mortality. Perhaps my friend Diane's recent death had something to do with it. Diane and I had been in Phoenix house together. After resuming contact with Beverli, I decided to see if I could get in touch with Diane as well. We were best friends in Phoenix House and stayed in touch for a while after we graduated but slowly went our separate ways, just living our lives.

Diane was half Italian and half German and just as neurotic as she wanted to be. During our time in rehab, we had a lot of fun criticizing and making fun of the other residents because we naively believed we didn't really belong there, with all those "drug addicts." We were two of the youngest residents in the house, only fourteen at the time, so folks didn't get too offended by our silliness. Anyway, after all those years, for some odd reason, I remembered her parents' phone number and was able to re-establish ties with her. She was married with no children and was mildly agoraphobic. We visited each other a few times over the years. She and her husband would host Christmas Eve, which was one of her greatest joys. Diane was an interior decorator, and their apartment was beautiful; she was her biggest client. We talked on the phone a lot, she drinking her vodka, I my cognac, and we analyzed ourselves, our relationships, and life. I remember one day telling her about my new relationship with Samantha.

"Diane," I began with great profundity, "I think I have abandonment issues."

Diane burst out laughing. "Oh, Mel, that's like you saying you just discovered you're Black."

I was perplexed, as this was news to me—the abandonment issue thing, that is, not being Black. But Diane had gone to therapy for years after Phoenix House, so she was perhaps more insightful than I. In retrospect, though, when I think about my relationships before Samantha, it was really quite obvious. I just hadn't put a label on it. Hmmm... was that what Maria meant when she said I was smothering her?

Diane began having serious problems in her marriage. She started drinking heavily in combination with taking prescription medication. She had near overdoses a couple of times. Then one night in August 2005, she called from a psych ward asking me for money for an attorney to get her out. I was frightened for her and suggested she stay for a while and get some rest. She got angry and hung up. When she was released shortly afterwards, I invited her to come and stay with me for a while in the country to regroup, as I had been doing all these past years. She declined. On September 5, 2005, her husband called. Diane was dead. Overdose. I was heartbroken.

During this period, Beverli's health issues were beginning to get the better of her as well. Her hospital stays became more frequent. She had blackouts, probably from the cancer spreading to her brain. My last visit with Beverli was October 5th, a month after Diane's death. It was Bev's birthday, and she was in the hospital again. Beverli was Jewish, and although she was not devout, she was not a believer in Jesus either.

Around this time, I was continually growing in my walk with Jesus, getting to know Him better. I regretted not knowing Him well enough before my brother died. I often feared that perhaps before Cliff died, he had not accepted Christ as his savior. Like I've said before, I'm not focused on the afterlife, but when one realizes that God is real and alive and instrumental in your life, well, it makes you pause sometimes, thinking about your deceased loved ones.

When I went to visit Beverli I was fully armed. I brought her a birthday card, a gospel CD, some religious pamphlets about receiving Christ, and my Bible from which I read Romans, chapter 10. Bev looked about a hundred years old, though she was only fifty-five. She was bald and toothless but remarkably sharp and strong spirited. Her will to live was tenacious and she said she didn't want to miss a thing. We discussed life, not sweating the small stuff and other related topics. Beverli died the following month.

Yup, it was time for me to start addressing my own health issues. I had my initial consultation at Westchester Medical Center on October 11, 2005. It was my first time going to this huge facility. Given a choice, this is where I would go for any kind of serious medical treatment. From what I've experienced, the medical care in the "country" leaves a lot to be desired. My gastroenterologist, who was an Orthodox Jew, seemed very competent. My primary physician informed me that I would need a liver biopsy. I wasn't too keen on that. I figured I needed every sliver of my liver, didn't have a piece to spare. However, the specialist informed me that with my type of hepatitis C, we could forego the biopsy and proceed with the treatment. Apparently, there are a few different genotypes of hepatitis C, and mine had been typically more responsive to treatment. Thank you Lord. We talked for a long time about various things. Dr. Isaacs set me at ease.

The next step was the intake nurse, Sonia, an Hispanic woman about my age. Sonia was to be my primary caretaker during the course of treatment. She had a small, shared office. We talked casually for a while. When Sonia asked me how I contracted the disease, I felt compelled to be honest with her. After all, she was to be my partner throughout this ordeal. When I told her that I was an IV user at the age of thirteen, I sensed a feeling of sorrow and pity coming from her. It made me feel pitiful and sad, too. Surely, she has heard this a thousand times before, so why should she feel sorry for me? Why should she have pity in her eyes for me?

Maybe, I was just perceiving her response that way. Perhaps, she had something else on her mind. After all, I know I mentioned I was a physical therapist and that I had a house in the Bahamas. Clearly, she could tell I was a woman of some affluence, not some drug addict. Hell, I don't even smoke cigarettes anymore. So, what's this look of pity about?

But like I said, it was probably coming from me. My past had come to haunt me, and the reality was I had been a drug addict. I did put needles in my arms and legs at the tender age of thirteen, and now I had to deal with the consequences of those actions. I guess that little wad of cotton that we used to put in the cooker to filter out impurities didn't quite do its job. I was feeling vulnerable and a little frightened. I was not comfortable being subject to the will of others. And being a health care professional, I had trust issues. Hell, I had trust issues regardless of the circumstances.

Sonia explained every detail of the treatment to me. She would get approval from my insurance company for the medication. The pharmacy would then mail the medication to my home on a monthly basis. "Uh, to my home? Don't I have to come in for my shots?" I was a bit confused.

"No," she answered kindly, "you will receive pills, Ribaviran, which you will take on a daily basis and the Interferon, which you will inject weekly. You must administer your injections on the same day every week, and try to do it around the same time."

She then informed me of the side effects I might expect, "The most common side effect is flu-like symptoms. You may feel a little feverish, a little lethargic, and maybe a little achy. You might have difficulty sleeping at times, and you may lose your appetite for a while. Sometimes, people experience mood changes or depression. Here's my card. Should you find yourself becoming unbearably depressed, or even if you just have any questions or concerns, please call me. We find

Tylenol works the best to relieve the flu-like symptoms. You will be on a three- month treatment program, after which time we hope your hepatitis will be gone. If not, then you will undergo treatments for an additional three months."

She was very professional yet kind and had a certain casual, matter of fact way about her that was reassuring without being cavalier. "As soon as I get the approval from your insurance company, I will contact you to schedule your first shot. You'll come back to me for that, at which time I'll instruct you on how to do it." I had to laugh to myself because back in the day, I was known as "the doctor." My fellow junkies used to ask me to hit them when they had difficulty finding a vein to inject. I could usually get the hit. Surely, I didn't need instructions to "skin pop," but that was another lifetime ago.

A bit concerned, I asked, "Is there a chance that the insurance company will deny me treatment?"

"There's always that possibility, but they usually approve it. Don't worry; if they deny you, we may have other avenues we can explore to provide treatment for you." Sonia smiled, "I'm going to send you to the lab now to get a blood work-up. We will also need a recent eye exam." Oh, did she neglect to tell me that Interferon causes blindness, too? Oh boy! I put Sonia's card carefully away in my purse and thanked her for her time and patience. "I'll be speaking with you soon." She patted me on the back as she walked me to the elevator.

The lab was in another building. As I walked across the campus, my head was spinning. So, I was really going through with this, eh? Damn right. I WANT TO LIVE! After walking for what seemed like a mile, I reached the building in which the medical laboratory was located. I handed my referral to the receptionist, who, a few minutes later, ushered me into a little booth. The laboratory technologist came in shortly afterwards. He was a very handsome Black man, perhaps a little younger than I. He introduced himself, explained the procedure, and set up his hypodermic and test tubes. While setting up, he engaged me in small talk and then looked at me and casually asked, "Are you on the program?" *What the hell program is he talking about?* I thought. I felt *less than*, small and embarrassed. Was my diagnosis on the referral? Of course, one of those tubes is for a viral load count. Did I look like an ex-addict? Did I sound like one? Well, I guess Mr. handsome lab technologist won't be asking me out on any dates. I was a patient now. That was my identity at Westchester Medical Center. I was on "the program."

During the hour and a half drive home, I found myself bursting into tears several times. It seems I had been doing that a lot over the past decade or so—actually over the past two decades. Wow! Later that evening, after dinner, I poured myself a drink, popped a bag of popcorn, and surfed the internet to get as much information about Interferon and Ribaviran as possible. It was time to face the truth and to face the pain without trying to dull it down because I only end up hurting myself more in the long run. That night I decided later for everyone and everything else. It was time to do me. I needed to focus entirely on my healing in every way. I committed myself to reading the Bible more, to truly making God my companion, and to just surrendering.

A certain peace began to overtake my spirit. I felt God was guiding my every step, and everything seemed to get just a little easier. From the simple day-to-day tasks to any greater challenges I was to face, I gave them to God and He took them. In my heart I knew that even if I did have to start treatments for the hepatitis (hoping for a spontaneous healing), I would be cured completely. I knew that it would be a time of growth, focus, and healing in many ways. Well, on October 28th I got my blood work results. I had minimal to no liver damage, Glory to God! My hepatitis C viral load dropped to 370,000 and everything else looked fine except my blood sugar, which was a bit high. That could be easily remedied through increased exercise and decreased sugar intake.

When I heard the news, I burst into tears and prayers of gratitude. My Father! I realized how much He does love me, and how He always protects me and delivers me. It became evident to me that He had something special for me to do for Him. That day, I began to develop a need to please Him. I felt so loved by Him. Ironically, that very morning, I was sarcastically saying to God that all I have is Him. And now, where would I be without Him? Our Father does have a sense of humor, you know.

The following week I got my eye exam. It was 20/20, so now I have all I need to begin the Interferon treatments. The pharmacy called to inform me that they had received my drugs and I was ready to go. The pharmacist assured me of the effectiveness of the drugs and offered the pharmacy's ongoing support. I got a bit teary-eyed. I know I'm a crybaby, okay. I thought, here we go, God be with me.

On November 29, 2005, I went down to Sonia's office to get my first shot. I brought my box of drugs with me that had been delivered the week before. I began taking the Ribavirin pills the day before the shot. Sonia and I talked together first. She asked how I was feeling, physically and emotionally. I jokingly said I already had a cold, so I probably wouldn't even notice the flu like symptoms. I think she could tell that I was emotionally shaken. She was sitting behind her desk, and I was at the side; no one else was in the office, and she had locked her door.

"Well, let's do this," she said. I had on jeans, so she gave me a gown to put over my lap and instructed me to pull my pants to my knees. She removed one of the syringes from the box. They were already pre-filled with the Interferon. There were four syringes in the box, a month's supply. She handed me the syringe and guided me in removing the cap, "Now, slowly push the plunger until you see some of the liquid drip from the needle, then stop." She watched me cautiously. My hand was trembling, as was my bottom lip. Tears started to roll down my face. I thought I would have been cooler, but I just broke down for some reason. Sonia handed me a tissue. "It's okay, you're doing fine. Hold the syringe firmly in your right hand so that you can push the plunger easily and smoothly. Now, pick a leg, pinch about an inch of flesh on your thigh, and hold it. Then put the needle in your thigh, let go of your flesh, and inject the medication."

It was as if I was kind of out of my body, just following instructions. I couldn't believe this was all happening. I was beginning to feel ashamed again with my pants down, sticking a needle in my thigh. But I did it. "Good, Melanie." She was encouraging. I gave her the empty hypodermic and pulled up my pants. She then advised me on proper disposal of the syringes and needles and gave me a red box for the used needles. She again implored me to call her if I had any difficulties at all. I thanked her. After a few minutes of idle chat, she asked if I was okay, to which I replied, "Yup."

She handed me my box of syringes, reminded me to refrigerate the medication, and take the shot each week on the same day. "That will be next Tuesday, okay, at about the same time, one o'clock." I assured her that I would follow her instructions without deviation. She walked me to the elevator. "See you soon, Melanie."

That night I felt okay; my cold was pretty bad, but I didn't have any additional symptoms. Maybe this ain't gonna be as bad as I anticipated. The next day, I started feeling a bit worse. I was very congested, and when I blew my nose, I could feel pressure in my neck and the back of my head.

Tuesday was approaching rapidly, and I was becoming

progressively irritable. There were the usual annoyances, the buildings and the tenants, but these days, I felt particularly agitated. It was shot time. I had a full breakfast that morning: eggs, bacon, toast, and coffee. I wasn't really hungry, but I didn't think I would have much of an appetite afterwards. I took my syringe from the refrigerator and sat at the kitchen table, waiting for the medication to get closer to room temperature. Wearing only a bathrobe, I sat, staring at my thigh. I could see the dark markings from last week's injection, which was one of the side effects.

My mind drifted back to the first time I ever injected myself with a hypodermic needle on the rear steps of Public School 20, the primary school I attended as a child. Regina and Douglas (my older, more experienced junkie friends) and I, all huddled in a circle, preparing to get high. Their instructions were much like Sonia's, detailed and given with concern. It was a summer, Saturday afternoon. Now, it's a wintery Tuesday. How ironic! A hypodermic needle, the very object that caused my life-threatening disease those many years ago, is now the tool I must use again to hopefully cure it. As I picked up the syringe and looked at my left thigh, it occurred to me that this was the same thigh I had shot into back then. I cleared the air from the syringe, pinched my thigh, wiped away a tear, and injected myself. I was so tense that I forgot to stop pinching as I injected, until blood oozed from the injection site, which prompted me to release my flesh. Well, most of the medicine got in.

As the weeks went on, administering the shots grew easier, but the side effects got worse. I was congested most of the time and feverish at night. The anticipated depression hadn't arrived yet, but I became increasingly petulant. My blood was monitored bi-weekly. Fortunately, I could have it drawn locally and didn't have to travel. That worked out well. It was getting cold, and all I really wanted to do was watch TV, sleep, self medicate (by that I do mean cognac), and recede into my abeyance. I had been taking aspirin for the flu symptoms until I decided to try the Tylenol that Sonia had initially suggested. It worked much better. Why must I so often insist on always doing things my way, instead of occasionally trusting others to know better?

My birthday and the holiday season were fast approaching. It was a pleasant diversion when some friends came over for dinner on my birthday. On December 20th, not three weeks after my first shot, I got a phone call from Sonia. My viral load had dropped from 370,000 to 3,459. She said that was very good! Praise God. Speaking of whom, before my treatments, I thought this would really be a great opportunity for me to grow closer to Him. I had begun Bible school in September but quit a few weeks into my treatment. My emotions about everything ranged from apathy to anger, and I had very little to give to others. Daily prayers and Bible readings didn't manifest the intimacy with God that I had anticipated. Yet in my heart, I knew that all was as it should be. I memorized Psalm 103:2, "Praise the Lord O my soul and forget not all His benefits. Who forgives all your sins and heals your diseases. Who redeems your life from destruction. Who crowns you with loving kindness and tender mercies." I prophesied this each and every day over myself. The new year would be better.

As the days progressed, I began to experience dizziness. One day, it was so bad that I called the fire department as I suspected there was a carbon monoxide leak. But it was nothing, just the medication. I also started getting nosebleeds. On one occasion, my nose gushed blood for at least an hour. I called the medical center and was advised to pinch my nostrils and hold my head back. Upon attempting this procedure, I almost drowned in my own blood when it drained down my throat. I was alone but didn't want to call an ambulance. The very thought of all that drama was a deterrent, and I really didn't want anyone touching me. I wasn't ready to be someone else's patient. Yes, once again, I felt sorry for myself, unable to even cry or I surely would have drowned in my blood and tears. Eventually, that bleeding episode came to an end. You know I was praying, right?

By the beginning of the new year, I began to pray and meditate on the Holy Spirit more often. In addition to my physical infirmities, at the properties, everything that could go wrong, did—there were broken pipes with leaks everywhere and my super quit. Next, the predicted depression began to set in. It was clear these events had a deeper meaning. A few months before, there was even a major flood at my home in the Bahamas. A hot water pipe had broken and filled the ground floor apartment. A friend of mine just happened to go in to check something, and as she opened the front door, the water came rushing out.

All the leaks and the blood flow indicated to me that something spiritual was going on. I searched my Bible for an answer. Seeking passages that pertained to running water led me to Isaiah 30:19, a scripture I had never read before, "O people of Zion who live in Jerusalem, you will weep no more. How gracious He will be when you cry for help. As soon as He hears you, He will answer you. Although the Lord gives you the bread of adversity and the water of affliction, your teachers will be hidden no more, with your own eyes you will see them. Whether you turn to the right or to the left, your ears will hear a voice behind you saying, this is the way, walk in it." What! With tear filled eyes, I appreciated more than ever before the great goodness of God. He hears me. He answers me. He cares for me and has shown me such love. I want to be obedient and know Him more and more. Thank You Lord. The following day Sonia called to inform me that my viral load was zero! Glory to God!

Oh, and Tommy, my sister's husband who had hepatitis C also? He made a remarkable recovery with medication and my sister's tender loving care, only to die a few years later due to hospital negligence while undergoing knee surgery. You just never know.

BOATING AND BETRAYAL

The year 2005 had been quite an eventful one. While in the Bahamas for the winter and spring, I completed my beach house dream: the purchase of a boat. My British friend Ron, a former boat owner, warned me against it, but the boat was a must have. It was an integral component to the whole living on the beach scenario. Ron used to say repeatedly, " A boat is a hole in the water that you throw money into." But I was determined to have the whole package, so I began my research.

Initially, a dinghy, which would have been a minimal investment, seemed adequate. Since I couldn't build a dock off my beach, I figured a dinghy would be most convenient, as I could just pull it ashore and tie it to the staircase of my sundeck. Upon further investigation I discovered that the average dinghy with an engine weighed a couple of hundred pounds, so there would be no pulling it ashore and tying it to the deck. First of all, I couldn't physically pull it ashore myself and then if I treated my deck like a dock, the ocean would soon claim it all.

So next, I considered a seventeen-foot boat. The Captain had a Boston Whaler, popular in Grand Cayman. In Exuma however, most of the newer boats seemed to be Twin Vees. I visited the docks on the island, looking at various boats. The Twin Vees were of particular interest because they had twin hulls, like catamarans, which made the ride much smoother, especially in rough waters.

Eventually, I met Johnny, one of the Twin Vee dealers on the island, a middle- age, White Bahamian—a proud, sun-burned man of the sea. He considered himself one of the top captains on the island. Johnny took me out on his twenty-six-foot, Twin-Vee. It was a beautiful ride, and he handled the boat flawlessly. This was exciting. This could soon be me. I looked online at all the available models. My dream grew larger and larger, as it went from seventeen feet to twenty feet, and then to a twenty-six footer that was a real beauty. It had a cabin with a head and a bed (toilet, sink and queen sized bed). She was fabulous, but twenty-six feet that was way too big. I discussed it with Johnny, who assured me if I could handle a seventeen footer, I could just as easily handle a twenty-six footer. He promised he would teach me everything I needed to know. This was do-able. I went to the website and started building my own boat with tank holders for scuba diving and rod holders for deep-sea fishing. She was going to be incredible!

My boat was shipped from Florida and trailered through town to the boatyard, impressing everyone who saw her. I asked Johnny to let me know when she was going to be launched. I wanted to be there; it was a spiritual thing. After some initial prep work and checks, she was ready. This was so exciting. When I arrived at the boatyard, she was attached to a crane. Johnny and I got on board, and the crane lifted us into the sea. It was a glorious moment. The "Thank You Lord" had been officially introduced to her new home, the ocean. Johnny started to pump something on the engine. Anxious to learn all that I could, I asked, "So Johnny, what are you doing now, priming the engines?"

Johnny screamed at me, "Melanie, Melanie, please!"

What the hell was that about? He's launched boats a

thousand times, so he can't be stressed. What the hell? "Look, man, don't stress me!" I snapped back. He had already ruined the moment. He kind of calmed down after that. My good friend Kersey told me in his very proper Bahamian accent that Johnny was really quite a character and that he was only being civil to make the sale of the boat. Was this true? We were both quiet after that. Johnny mumbled some excuse about the launch being tricky, etc., but I was beginning to see his true colors. On the way to the slip where the boat would be docked, he began to show me a few basic things: the ignition, the throttle, and the gas gauge. I operated the boat for a few minutes, and then we pulled into the dock.

My boat was docked in a gated community. Johnny was the harbormaster there, and because it was a very exclusive property, she was safe. There were quite a few Twin Vees docked there, but the Thank You Lord was by far the grandest. After we docked, I asked Johnny when my first lesson would be. He grumbled something about calling me, but he didn't make a definite plan. This was a hostile man. Why didn't I see it before?

"You need to go to the office to register the boat and pay the dockage fees," he said, "five hundred dollars a month." I hadn't anticipated that.

Later that evening, I went to Kersey's house to tell him of my adventure and have a few glasses of wine.

"I told you!" he said.

"Yes dear, it seems you were right." I sighed.

The next morning, I waited to hear from Johnny. He never called. The following day, when I still hadn't heard from him, I decided to go to the boat anyway and acquaint myself with the Thank You Lord. She was so big and pretty. I dropped the engines, turned on the ignition, and experimented with the GPS. I went into the cabin, looked around, turned on the light, flushed the toilet, turned on the short-wave radio, and listened to some other boaters. I watched people bringing their boats in and out of the docking area. Then I turned off the power and went home.

Before I got my boat, another friend Bobby told me he would go boating with me. He had a Twin Vee also and told me he would teach me all the tricks of maneuvering the boat. But when my boat was afloat, suddenly no one was available. Kersey, my closest friend on Exuma, avoided even going to see the boat. In fact, after a few glasses of wine in the evenings, he'd talk about how he was going to get himself a fully crewed yacht.

Through much persistence on my part, I finally got Johnny to take me out again for another lesson. He drove out into the middle of the harbor, gave me the controls, and then shouted, "Steer right, steer left, hold your course, hold your course!" By our third time out together, it was evident this arrangement was not going to work. He didn't allow me to ask any questions. He just took me out, barked orders, and then we docked. I didn't sign up for this!

When we got to the dock, before we disembarked, Johnny began to read me the riot act, "I don't know what your problem is. I think you have a problem with authority. But let me tell you, I've been to the White House. I have taught the President of General Motors how to captain a boat. I..." He continued his tirade for what seemed like hours, but I was cool. I held my tongue, picked up my bottle of water, took a sip, and listened to him. I'm sure my face must have turned red, 'cause inside I was livid. When he finished his verbal rampage, I took a deep breath, had another sip of water, and exercised self-control beyond my known capabilities. Because he was the harbormaster and I knew I would probably need him in the future with matters pertaining to the boat, I couldn't afford to completely alienate him or the scenario would have gone quite differently. (I wasn't as holy then as I am now.)

"Johnny," I said slowly and calmly, "No doubt, you are a very knowledgeable sea captain, and your time and efforts are truly appreciated, but I got it from here. I won't be needing your instruction anymore, okay? Thanks so much." He looked a bit shocked. Yeah, man, I don't know what your problem is, but you won't be abusing me anymore! Of course, I only thought that part; I didn't say it out loud.

Now I'm on my own. The next morning, I went to the dock, which was in town about a half hour drive, and proceeded to teach myself how to handle the boat. It was quite intimidating, but I was determined not to let Johnny destroy my dream. That day, I boarded the boat and just looked around, familiarizing myself with my surroundings. There were at least twenty other boats docked at this pier. My slip was at the far end of the pier and relatively easy to get in and out. I didn't have to maneuver around any other boats, just backing up and pulling out was all that was required. I began practicing. I dropped my engines and started them, untied the boat from the dock, pushed the throttle slowly in reverse, and then inched her forward. Each time I would go back a little further and then forward. Soon I felt confident enough to pull her out of the pier altogether. Getting into the harbor was tricky, though. I had to consider the wind and the tide and avoid the shallows where sand could get into the engines, all the while being aware of the rocky jetty that protruded out to the entrance. But I did it. The heat of the sun relaxed my body as I pushed the throttle forward. The azure sky was decorated with billowing, white clouds and giant sails from the surrounding, anchored boats. And at the horizon, the sky seemed to become one with the sea. The scent of the salt air beckoned me further out into the ocean.

Entering the harbor, one needed to be aware of the

anchor lines of the other boats so as not to get ensnared in them. Elizabeth Harbor is fifteen miles long and hosts many yachtsman and boaters for the winter. It is stunning, with crystal clear waters that are so typical throughout the Bahamas. And once I reached the middle of the harbor, it was smooth sailing. Trying to avoid any passing boats or ships, while being aware of my compass and direction, I would drive up and down, steering to the right and to the left.

My iPod was playing some fabulous music, which always enhances everything for me. I started to feel the exhilaration of driving a boat, cutting through the water with a rooster tail following (the shape of the water formed by the engines at the back of the boat). It was breathtaking! Now that's what I'm talking about! I drove around the harbor for a couple of hours, thinking how cool it was, but as I began to head for the pier, my stomach knotted up. Now came the hard part, docking. Okay, Johnny said to slow down once you passed the jetty, and so I did, almost to a crawl. I prayed that no one was on the pier; in case I messed up, I didn't want to look like a fool. Needing to focus, I turned off my iPod. My mouth was dry, my heart was pounding and I was a little shaky. God, I can't wait to have a drink after this.

Getting into the slip required making kind of a u-turn around the pier, but I hadn't ever practiced that move. There wasn't much space to make the u-turn because there was land to the rear of the dock, and each slip was assigned two boats. Johnny shared a slip with me, but fortunately, his boat wasn't there. I tried to make a wide enough turn to give myself the time and space needed to get her lined up just right to pull into the slip. I slowed down as much as possible. Evidently I was too slow because before I could grab a line and tie up, the wind pushed me away from the pier. Ughhh... Thank God Johnny's boat wasn't there. I had to back her up again and try to pull back to the dock. I realized that in order to counteract the force of the wind, I had to give her more juice to direct her closer to the pier. The front of my boat banged into the pier, but at least I got close enough to grab a line and secure it to the center cleat to keep her in place. Praise the Lord! I was so stressed I didn't even notice if anyone was around me. After getting her secured, I rinsed her off and went home for a much-deserved cocktail. No wonder sea captains are notorious for drinking—it's stressful out there. I'm feeling anxious just recalling the incident.

The second time I went boating by myself, the anxiety began to build from the moment I woke up. Had my dream turned into a nightmare? All the way to the pier, I prayed and reassured myself I could do this. At the dock, there were people coming and going or just lingering around. Oh boy, now I had an audience! And to top it off, Johnny's boat was in the slip. Ughhh...

I tried to gather all my reserve. It was obvious I was a novice, and my boat was the most impressive on the pier. You know everyone had been talking about it, right? There goes that Black American woman who owns the new Twin Vee with the cabin. No one else with a Twin Vee had a cabin, not even Johnny. And now, they're all looking at me, watching and waiting for me to make a fool of myself or wreck my boat. I walked down the pier with a smile and said hey to every one who acknowledged me. My mouth was getting dry again, and my legs felt as if I were already on the water. It was terrible.

Upon boarding the boat, I tried to remember the sequence of everything I was supposed to do. First, check the radio, make sure it's working. Turn on the GPS. Unlock the cabin door and stow your gear (getting the nautical terminology down, at least). Okay, drop the engines, straighten out your wheel, and then turn the engines on. All systems operating? Oh boy, here we go. It was too early to put my music on because I still needed to focus. Time to untie the boat. Oh, which way is the wind blowing? I left one of the lines in easy access so that upon my return, I could reach it as soon as the boat neared the dock. I put the throttle in reverse with just enough speed not to drift into Johnny's boat, heaven forbid, and I backed up. Once clearing the pier, I pushed her forward, and away we went. When I reached open water, I put on my music, went into the cabin and got a beer (came prepared). It was party time. I went from one end of the harbor to the other. Johnny had warned me never to exit the harbor from the northwest channel as it was very challenging, so I steered clear. I drove up and down and around the harbor, listening to music, drinking beer, and having a grand time. I even pulled near the shore and practiced dropping anchor and pulling it back up. I was getting the hang of using the compass and staying on course, but the GPS, quite frankly, remained a mystery to me.

After a couple of hours of ecstasy, the dreaded task of returning to the dock at Exuma Manors was at hand. Exuma Manors is located at the eastern part of the harbor. Upon approaching the piers, I could see the grand houses that adorned the shoreline. As I got closer, I spied the little, rocky jetty. Time to slow down. The piers were shaped in a kind of squared S formation. My slip was the first one, the easiest to get into, located at the top of the S. All I had to do was drive straight up the side of the piers and make my U-turn. As I approached the jetty, my little beer buzz was immediately replaced by a faint nausea. I turned off the music and cautiously approached the dock. Oh, no, Johnny's boat was still there. My anxiety heightened. I made the U-turn and thought my approach was looking good. All of a sudden, Johnny came running down the pier, screaming at me. I didn't know what the hell he was screaming about, but it totally threw off my focus. I tried to concentrate and bring her in straight and near to the dock so I could grab my line and cut my engines, but he was still screaming. I got to the dock, held on to my line and began to pull the boat towards the dock, so I could secure her. In all the confusion, however, the throttle was in reverse, so the boat was pulling against me. Johnny then screamed, "You're in reverse!"

I pushed the throttle to neutral and got the line into the cleat. My hands were shaking. Johnny rambled on about something, I don't know what he was saying, but I did know this would be the last time he humiliated me. What the hell! What was his plan? Perhaps he wanted to make my boating experience so miserable that I would sell the boat back to him at a deep discount, so he could re-sell it? If I were a White male, he wouldn't be treating me like this. What's wrong with this man?

I got my boat squared away, and when I disembarked, Johnny was on the pier. Now, I'm pissed! This time, I approached him with a certain amount of aggression. "Johnny, let me tell you something. Unless you see me about to kill someone, or kill myself, don't say a word to me while I'm on my boat. I don't know what it is about you, but you stress me out, man. Maybe, it's a father thing."

He interrupted, "A father thing? I'm not old enough to be your father."

You look old enough to be my father, you sunburnt, miserable ... I thought but did not say. You get my gist, right? "Just stay away from me Johnny, okay."

He grumbled okay or something and went on his not so merry way.

That year, 2005, the first year of my boat ownership, I continued to go out by myself. I even ventured out of the harbor, on the southeast side, as recommended by you know who, but going in and out of the dock was still a dreaded task for me. One day towards the end of my stay in Exuma, I was pulling into the dock with my usual trepidation, but my execution was perfect. As I secured my first line, heeeres Johnny! Does this guy have *me* on his GPS? He's always around.

He actually smiled. "We've got to get you a captain's hat."

What? A smile and a word of approval! Curiously enough, it was very satisfying to get Johnny's approval. It must be kind of like when someone is holding you prisoner, and after a while, you come to love your captor. What's it called, Stockholm syndrome? Not that I was feeling any love for Johnny, but still, his approval suddenly meant a lot to me. Hmmm. But I was cool. I just replied, "Already got one."

The following year, I was demoted in my docking status. Instead of being in the elite, easy to dock section, I was in the middle of the S. That meant that in addition to sharing a slip with another boat, there were boats close behind me and to either side of me. I had to back up and turn in order to angle my boat perpendicular to the slip without backing into someone's boat or hitting the boat next to me. Then I had to straighten out, drive my boat past the other boats, and turn again around the end of the pier without coming too close to the rocky shore before I could head out past the jetty. When I saw where my boat was docked, a pang of panic shot through me. Oh, man. Plus, there were other boaters around. Oh no way, no way could I do this. I went to the office to see if my slip could be changed. My boat was dead center in the pier, the absolute most difficult spot from which to pull out. I bet Captain Johnny had something to do with this. Got your own hat, eh? There was no one in the office. I got into my car and drove home, feeling very defeated.

The next morning I prayed for a windy day. When it's windy and the ocean is choppy or unsettled, most Bahamians don't go boating. Then at least my friends and acquaintances wouldn't be smugly asking, "Did you go out on your boat today?" Each morning, I woke up with anxiety and prayed for heavy winds. The dream *had* turned into a nightmare. But then the winds dropped, and I had no excuse. Now as I write this, I know what you must be thinking. Why didn't she just hire someone to teach her how to use her boat? And you're absolutely right. Surely, there were plenty of unemployed captains around town. I considered it, but it seemed very costly, and I felt as if I was being taken advantage of, compounded with already feeling victimized and disappointed by Johnny. In my mind, I was all alone in this endeavor. Sometimes I think our brains get fixed in a certain mode, a certain perception of how things should be, and then we can't really see beyond that. You know what I mean, like tunnel-vision?

Anyway, this particular morning, the winds had dropped. It was a fair day, good enough for boating. I gathered my resolve and headed to the pier. There were others on the dock again but no sign of Johnny, a real plus. I fumbled

My boat in dock.
(Everyone else is out to sea.)

with the radio and GPS and then decided to see if someone was in the office. I wanted to try, once more, to get an easier slip from which to maneuver. The manager, Rick, was there. Great. He seemed pleasant enough. When I asked him about changing slips, he informed me that there weren't any available. Rick was a young man. I had seen him around town at some of the clubs and partying on his boat.

"Come on man," I urged, "there must be something better. I'm new at this and I can't get out of that slip."

Rick smiled. "There's nothing to it. When I first started boating, I didn't know what I was doing either. Still don't. Just do it, you'll be all right."

Oddly enough, his words did give me some encouragement. I didn't feel like the only novice on the sea. These were the first words of actual encouragement I had received since I got my boat. I went back to the boat, clenched my jaw, and pulled out without any trouble whatsoever, aside from almost having a heart attack. I did my routine in the harbor, came back to the slip with my usual dread and anxiety, and docked just fine.

The next morning as I lay in bed, wishing for the winds and rough sea, I had to really analyze the situation. What was I so afraid of? Certainly I wasn't afraid of being on the ocean. I wasn't afraid of killing anyone or being killed while boating. No fear of sharks attacking the boat and eating me alive. So, what was all this anxiety about? What was the root? Then I started wishing I had somewhere else to dock, somewhere without all those people watching and waiting for me to make a mistake. Oh my goodness, could it be that all this anxiety and fear had nothing to do with boating? Undeniably, it was pure ego, pure vanity. I wasn't afraid of any boating mishaps for the danger of it all. I just didn't want to look bad. Really, was I that vain? Apparently so, I had to laugh at myself. In Proverbs, the Bible tells us, "Pride goes before destruction, a haughty spirit before a fall." Surely, my pride was destroying my whole boating experience. Wow!

After that revelation, I would like to say my anxiety immediately decreased and taking the boat out got easier, but no, not immediately. My confidence gradually grew, or I should say my haughty spirit very gradually began to diminish. This was to be only the beginning of the revelation of how prideful I really was. My friend's brother, Vernal, began accompanying me on the boat. We would go fishing. Vernal was about seventy or so and had greatly diminished vision. I used to call him Mr. Magoo. But he was helpful and easy to be with, and at least, he was available.

I also observed the other boaters more keenly. None of them were experts although some were better than others. I think everyone had a little angst about their performance when people were watching. There was kind of a boating hierarchy at the pier. The seasoned captains usually sped into the dock with confidence and pizzazz. The others tried to look confident, but they had no real pizzazz in their docking, and you could see the relief on their faces when they got a line secured and were able to cut their engines. On board, both the experienced and inexperienced had two things in common—alcohol and a companion. Both were of invaluable assistance. Now I had Vernal and a cooler full of Kaliks (Bahamian beer). I even ventured out of the harbor from the northwest channel, the one I was warned to avoid at all costs, and I did it without incident although it was tricky. Yes, I was getting better.

STRANDED

When I returned to the Bahamas in the winter of 2007, my head was not in the best of places. I was journeying deeper into my spirituality and had become more committed to my walk with God. I joined a Pentecostal church in Poughkeepsie, N.Y. and was baptized just before I returned to the Bahamas. As I may or may not have previously mentioned, I am not devoted to any one religion. Jesus died for us to have a relationship with our Father. He didn't die for us to have a religion. But the pastor of this particular church spoke to me, or should I say, God spoke to me through him. It was amazing. More often than not, there were mornings that I would pray about something and it would be the exact thing pastor would preach on that Sunday. Incredible! God really does speak to me. He really does care. The church was Spirit filled, and I was inspired to attend regularly.

I had been asking God for revelation, to show me where I was falling short and needed to grow. I used to half joke that if it weren't for my drinking, I'd be perfect, so alcohol must be the "thorn in my side" to keep me humble. I say half joke because part of me did believe it to be so. Boy, was I wrong. It's like when I was sixteen and thought I knew it all, and no one could tell me anything. When I turned forty, I discovered I knew nothing. In addition to this process of self-actualization, I was becoming acutely aware of how isolated I was upstate. The community's populace was predominantly lower to middle class White folks whose exposure for the most part did not exceed the county's borders. Here, people my age had long since been married to their high school sweethearts, and there was not much of a gay community within a seventy-mile radius. My family lived eighty miles to the north and to the south and I had no friends in the immediate area. I had more of a social life during the three to four months that I spent in the Bahamas than I did the remainder of the year in New York.

Upon my arrival in Exuma that winter, my housekeeper informed me that while cleaning downstairs she saw a big rat run from the bedroom to the hall closet. She was Jamaican, and I'm sure she had seen some rats in her day, so when she described it as a *big rat*, I knew it was something to be reckoned with. She then showed me how it had eaten the bottom of the wooden closet door. This was serious.

Now, at home in the country, I dealt with field mice, which were actually kind of cute. Outside, there were groundhogs that I used to shoot, raccoons, possums, foxes, and coyotes, etc., the key word being, *outside*. I don't do rats, especially not big rats. And even though I inhabit the second story of the house, I did not sleep well that night or many nights to follow.

I put poison throughout the downstairs part of the house. Although it ate some of the poison, there was no body to be found. My friend came and put down a couple of big rattraps. No rat. I couldn't rest as I began to develop an irrational fear of this rodent. The rat was in my head. I told a friend of mine about my fear and obsession and how I couldn't sleep. She told me that when she had something on her mind, bothering her, eating away at her and she couldn't quite put her finger on it, she called it "the rat." Interesting, but my rat was flesh and blood and teeth, not metaphorical.

Clearly, though, I was battling more than one kind of rat. There was the physical one downstairs, but there were also a few upstairs, in my mind. One night the devil woke me up laughing. With a Bahamian accent, he said, "Yeah, you put down poison to kill the rat, and he went into the cistern (the entrance to which was behind the half eaten door) and poisoned your water, so now, you gonna die."

After that, I did get sick for a while with stomach pains. I don't think the rat could have actually gotten into the cistern, but I was under attack, spiritual attack from the enemy. Ephesians 6:12 tells us, "For our struggle is not against flesh and blood, but against the rulers, against the authorities, against the powers of this dark world and against the spiritual forces of evil in the heavenly realms."

It seemed everything that could go wrong, did go wrong. But I belonged to a church, and I was baptized, so wasn't everything supposed to be right and good in my life now, no? Instead, I was a wreck. But that's Satan's ploy. John 10:10 states, "The enemy comes only to steal, kill and destroy: I have come that they may have life, and have it to the full." Satan was stealing my peace of mind and trying to destroy my faith. Sometimes, the closer you get to a break-through, I mean some real progress, that's when the enemy pulls out all the stops. I never found the rat's dead body, but I found his entrance and sealed it up. I haven't had a rat in the house since. Oh, and obviously I didn't die, so...the devil is a liar!

It had been pretty windy since my arrival in Exuma, so I had not gone out on the boat. Eventually, the weather cleared, and I was ready for my maiden voyage of the season. I decided to go it alone, listen to some music, maybe anchor on one of the cays or along the shoreline somewhere, and clean the bottom of my boat. With Kalik in hand and headphones in my ears, I headed out of the harbor and decided to go to Pigeon Cay. On my way south, I saw some of my friends in their boat, a much smaller craft. As we passed one another, I looked *down*, saluted them with my beer, and kept on going. The wind and the water were fairly calm. All was well.

Pigeon Cay is a good way south of the harbor, but not too far from my home. I can see it from my balcony. I had never gone to Pigeon Cay alone, so this was to be a new adventure. I approached the cay from the south side, where there is a beautiful beach. There's nothing much to it, just a small, uninhabited cay. I pulled up as close as I could safely get, listening to my music and feeling pretty confident. I cut the engines and raised them a bit. I then went to the bow, singing along with my iPod, to drop anchor. As soon as the anchor dropped, BOOM, a wave crashed against the side of my boat. I turned around to see what happened. Boom, another wave and the stern of my boat was sitting on top of the beach. It's funny how the winds can shift, and the tides can turn on you in the blink of an eye. I couldn't believe it. I ran to the stern of the boat and jumped down to assess the situation. Boom, another wave, and the music stopped. That was the second iPod I had lost this trip. I had just purchased this iPod for three hundred dollars plus shipping and one hundred and fifty dollars in import duty. Damn!

Anyway, I had more important matters at hand. I threw the iPod on board and just stood there as the waves kept coming, one after another, pounding my boat further and further up on the beach. I tried lifting the stern of the boat when the waves came, hoping to catch a wave and have the stern carried back into the water. Did I mention it was a twenty-six-foot boat with two 140 hp Suzuki engines which probably weigh three hundred pounds a piece, not to mention the weight of the boat itself? What was I thinking? Obviously, I was in shock! I climbed aboard the boat. It was about 2 p.m. Okay, let me think. I could radio someone to come and help me, but then everyone would know that I got shipwrecked. I'd be the laughing stock of the island. Nah, someone will pass by. I'll flag them down, and they can just tow me off the cay. No one will have to know.

I got off the boat and walked the beach trying to make sight of another boat. I walked to the top of the cay. No boats in sight. I went back to my boat and tried to fix an anchor line to the stern, somehow hoping to have the tide pull the boat back out into the ocean. It wasn't happening. Then, in the distance, I spotted a small craft. Grabbing the gaff that was on board, I tore off my shirt, went to the shoreline, and waved my flag furiously while shouting to them, but to no avail. I got back on board the boat. What's going on? It was almost 3 p.m. and would soon be dark. It was time to get on the radio and find someone to tow me. Time to put my pride aside (told you I hadn't completely subjugated that monster yet). I picked up the transmitter and turned to channel 16, the call and distress channel. I pressed the talk button. "This is the Thank You Lord, I'm beached over on Pigeon Cay and need someone to tow me off. Come in, please." I tried to sound as cool and collected as possible. No big thing, nothin' to talk about.

No response.

I tried again. Again, no response. The radio was silent, despite my numerous requests for help.

I stopped asking to be towed, which was perhaps asking too much, and possibly why no one was responding. "Hey, this is the Thank You Lord. I'm shipwrecked on Pigeon Cay and need someone to come get me. Come in, please." There was a bit more desperation in my voice but still, no response. What! Every time I left the harbor, I checked the radio. Now, when I need it, it's not working! What in hell is going on? Desperately reading the manual for the radio, I started taking it apart but quickly put it back together, determining there was nothing wrong with it. Wait, there's another boat in the distance. I pulled off my shirt again, put it on the gaff, waved and shouted with even more fervor than previously. Wasn't so proud now, standing on the beach topless, screaming for help. They were too far away and didn't see or hear me. I went back on board and again attempted to hail someone. Still no response.

It was approaching 4 p.m., and I was beginning to get upset. I regained some composure and got back on the radio. Maybe if I'm more entertaining someone will respond. I started singing the lyrics to Pink Floyd's, "Comfortably Numb." "Hello, is anybody in there?" NOTHING! I started to cry. "Come on now, get yourself together," my voice of reason attempted to calm me. "It's gonna be all right. You have a half-gallon of water and an apple. You can sleep in your wet suit for protection, and at least, you have a cabin. You can make it through the night."

Mellie cried back, "I don't even have any music."

"There's a light in the cabin, so you can read."

"Read what, the radio manual?" Mellie sarcastically retorted.

I began to cry again.

"Come on, it's an adventure, like Gilligan's Island." Rational me began to sing, "A three hour tour, a three hour tour." I thought, "It'll be a good story to tell someday, and tomorrow some boats will pass by and pick you up." Then I remembered the weather forecast. Tomorrow was supposed to be rainy and windy. So if no one is out here now, ain't nobody gonna be out here tomorrow.

I broke down in tears. "God, what is going on? Am I doing something wrong? Is there something I'm not seeing that I need to be doing? Why is everything going wrong? Are you angry with me? Please help me, and if I'm doing something wrong, show me, so I can do better, please, God."My voice of reason tried to console and compose me again, "It's all right. You have your snorkel gear on board. If no one comes, you can just snorkel home in the morning." I could see my house from the boat, so near yet so far, maybe about a mile or two away. "Yeah, you could just snorkel from rock to rock until you get to your beach. You can do it."

Pigeon Cay from my Balcony

"Oh, Hell no!" I decided. "I'm not gonna be shark breakfast, snorkeling home. That's insane. And I don't want to spend the night on this boat to be dinner for the noseeums, either. I want to go HOME! I need a drink and the liquor store is going to be closed soon. I've got to get out of here!" I jumped back on the radio. "This is the Thank You Lord. Come in, please, come in, please. I'm stranded on Pigeon Cay." Again, nothing. I jumped off the boat, pushed and pulled it. The sun would be setting very soon.

"Thank You Lord, come in, please." The radio! I jumped back on board, almost breaking my ankle in my haste.

"This is the Thank You Lord. Come in, please," my voice quavered.

"Hi, I heard your message, but I'm not on a boat. I think I'm your neighbor." It was a man's voice.

"My neighbor?"

"Yeah, we're staying in Andy and Karen's house." I did recall seeing a couple at my neighbor's house, but they hardly came out. I assumed they were on their honeymoon or something and spent most of their time in the bedroom.

"Yeah, we just happened to have had the shortwave radio on, and as I was coming out of the bedroom, I heard your message. Who should I call to come get you?"

God had heard me! "Call Johnny." I knew his number by heart.

"Okay, hold on." He returned shortly, "Okay, I got him. He's on his way. I'll stay on the line with you until he get's there, okay? My name is Jim."

"Okay, thanks Jim. I'm Melanie."

I started gathering my gear together, so I would be ready when Johnny arrived. I secured the boat to the best of my ability, so he wouldn't have anything extra to do aside from coming to my rescue. And why shouldn't he come to my rescue? It was his damn fault that I was out here stranded in the first place. If he had kept his word and instructed me as he had promised, perhaps I would have done something differently and I wouldn't have been in this predicament to begin with. But, hey, stuff happens, and I believe almost everything happens for a reason. There is a lesson to be learned from all our experiences if we're receptive and acknowledge our share of responsibility in all circumstances.

Well, might as well prepare yourself to be yelled at today, I thought as I packed my waterlogged iPod in my bag with the rest of my things. Whatever, as long as I get to sleep in my bed tonight. I looked over at my house again. Be home soon, girl. Johnny's boat was rapidly approaching. Here we go. He pulled up near the shore, threw me a line, instructed me to attach it to the front cleat, and he secured another anchor to my boat. After we finished securing the boat, I grabbed my gear and waded through the water to board his boat. He didn't say a word. With a shaky, tearful voice (even though the last thing I wanted was for Johnny to see me cry), I said, "So Johnny, you want to yell at me now or later?"

"Nah, just as long as you're safe. There's some juice and soda in the cooler," was his gruff reply.

"No, thanks, I need a real drink about now." The sun was just beginning to set as we entered the harbor. "Wow, the sunset is surely beautiful today, but if it weren't for you, I'd be standing on my boat, watching this beautiful sunset and crying my eyes out. Thank you for coming to get me." A few tears did escape and make their way down my cheek, but Johnny's back was to me, thank goodness. He didn't reply. When we got to the dock, I sincerely thanked him again, hugged him, and told him I wanted to take him to dinner as a gesture of my appreciation. He agreed.

On the way home, since the liquor store was closed, I stopped at my neighborhood bar to have a much needed, stiff drink. There were a few guys hanging out, including Richie, who had built my house. I told them of my escapade, since word was going to get out, one way or the other, on this small island. Each one had a story to tell of being stranded, or shipwrecked, or some kind of nautical mishap. It occurred to me, it's all part of the boating experience. The ocean is no joke and deserves much respect.

After a few drinks and a few stories, my humiliation began to dissipate. The next day, I told my good friend Nancy, another winter resident. Nancy has been coming here for many decades and knows a lot of people, so I knew the cat would be out of the bag once I told her. It didn't matter now. Next thing I knew, Nancy had planned a dinner party around my adventure. She invited some of her acquaintances, boaters who were living in the harbor. I invited Johnny, and we all met at a restaurant in town.

While sharing my story during dinner, it occurred to me, these are the very people who didn't answer my distress calls. "Aren't boaters kind of obligated to respond to another vessel in distress? Isn't that part of the rules of the sea?" I asked.

Someone asked what kind of radio and antenna I had.

"Just a regular VHF radio. My antenna ranges about two or three feet off the bimini top," I replied.

"Oh, well that's the problem. You weren't within line of sight," was the response.

"Line of sight, what do you mean?" I wondered what sight had to do with my radio.

"If your boat can't be seen, your radio with a regular antenna can't be heard. No one heard you. That's why no one responded to your distress calls."

"Oh, I didn't know that." I looked accusatorily at Johnny.

"That's why I always carry my cell phone," he chimed in. That would have been a useful tidbit of information, ya think? Johnny may be an exemplary sea captain, but his teaching skills left a lot to be desired. So... that's why my neighbor heard me, because I was in his line of sight. I could see my house from Pigeon Cay, and they were just next-door. Johnny must have realized that night that he hadn't done right by me because *he* paid for our dinner and then hurried off. I followed him, gave him a hug, and thanked him again for everything. I didn't go boating anymore that trip; it was almost time to leave anyway.

When I returned to New York and to my home in the wilderness, while praying one morning, I received a revelation: My boat's being "beached" on Pigeon Cay was a metaphor of my life. I was beached! From the time I had lost my physical therapy practice and left the city, I'd been set adrift, subject to the winds, with no particular direction. I was washed ashore, stranded, just like on Pigeon Cay. I had avoided openly asking for help. Was I too proud, or had this been my behavior throughout my life—never wanting to expose myself or to show vulnerability and never feeling comfortable asking or depending on anyone for help?

It became clear that I needed help on so many levels. I could no longer afford to be proud, or afraid of rejection, or untrusting, or unworthy. I had to shout it out, get on the transmitter and scream H-E-L-P, even if that help comes from the last person on earth from whom I would want to ask it. Also, I must not forget the "line of sight" rule. Only those who can see you will hear you. It was time for me to get out there and be seen and heard.

Linda had recently told me that I must figure out how to get back out into the world and start socializing again. Initially, I felt a little resentful and depressed. She saw my isolation and my vulnerability. Did I really think it wasn't obvious? I was always acting as if I had it all together, when, in actuality, I was falling apart. Everything happens for a reason! Find the lesson. God was humbling me, exposing me to myself. You cannot conquer what you don't confront. Thank You Lord. And I gotta tell you, the Lord seems to deal with me pretty swiftly. When I am doing something contrary to my spirit, to the Holy Spirit within, I receive conviction almost immediately. Walking in the spirit and being responsive to the conviction is entirely another story.

I'm glad that God has not given up on me and that He cares enough to show me where and how I am less than I could be, not less than what others think I should be but less than I have the God-given potential to be. And I am so thankful that He has given me the time to grow. It is a blessing.

Last year, I was dating a lady who loved TV. Though she lived in a one-bedroom apartment, she had a sixty-inch TV in her living room. I don't think I had ever experienced a sixty-inch screen that close. It was huge and vivid and awesome. I like TV myself, Jackie liked TV, and I liked Jackie, so I wanted to accommodate her when she came to visit. I wanted her to feel comfortable and at home. So, I decided to get a larger TV for the basement.

Soon after I purchased the house in 1994, I discovered I had a wet basement. I thought I had remedied the problem through a company that guaranteed my basement would be dry when they finished the job. They jack-hammered around the perimeter of two of the walls and set up a drainage system. I had new flooring and carpeting installed. The basement was furnished with an old leather sectional set that I brought from my apartment in the Bronx.

Throughout the years, the basement always had a slight mildew odor. At times, I used a dehumidifier, but I just accepted the odor as normal for a basement. The smell was of no real consequence to me and when needed, Glade plug-ins or air fresheners would mask the odor adequately.

The purchase of the new TV had a snowball effect. I needed speakers and a sub-woofer for surround sound, and hey, might as well get some new furniture, something big and comfortable and soft, so Jackie and I could snuggle up and watch TV. Upon removing the old couch, I discovered the basement was still wet. The carpeting in the corner was soaked, and there were water stains on the paneling behind the couch. I immediately called the waterproofing company to hold them to their warranty. They informed me that I would have to remove the paneling from the wall and the carpeting from the floor, so they could do an inspection and find the source of the problem. "*I* have to remove the paneling and carpeting? Isn't that *your* responsibility according to your warranty?" The answer was negative. I consulted my attorney, and as all that was not specified in the contract, they were not responsible. So, I hired someone to remove and discard the paneling on the two wet walls, and lo and behold, there were thousands of carpenter ants nesting behind the paneling. I had often seen carpenter ants outside on the deck during the summer, and at times, I even spotted some inside. The house had been exterminated, but again, I just thought it was part and parcel of country life. No major problem, nothing out of the ordinary. Mind you, my house is predominantly wood, inside and out. In addition to the nesting ants, which we sprayed and stomped furiously, there was mold and mildew. So now I had to engage a mold company to treat the basement. In the meantime, my basement was completely decimated. The exposed walls were mold-covered cinderblock. The carpeting was rolled back halfway across the room and my new TV and furniture were all pushed into the far corner, covered in plastic, just one big mess.

When the representative from the waterproofing company came, he determined that the water was coming through the wall from the ground outside, but they were not responsible because they didn't waterproof the walls, just the floors, so it would be an additional fifteen hundred dollars for the walls. What? Shouldn't they have anticipated that? Didn't waterproofing my basement include the walls? Well, annoyed as I was, I wasn't going to hire another company because then the warranty would have been totally invalidated. If I took them to court, my basement would be a disaster area for months. So, we worked out a compromise. After they completed the work, I could always take them to court to recoup my eleven hundred dollars, the amount we settled on. I never bothered with legal action though, again, the peace of mind factor. Plus, it was partially my fault because the gutters were extremely clogged, causing water to pour out and settle on the ground beside the wet wall. So, one thing led to another, to another, and to yet another. Had I not removed the couch, the paneling, and the carpeting, I would never have discovered how serious and how perilous the underlying problem was.

How often do we coif our hair, put on some pretty clothing, and splash on some cologne, yet, just beneath the surface, there's some ugly, stinking, destructive stuff going on? I had all the warning signs but ignored the symptoms, dismissing them as "the norm." Sometimes, before we start dressing up, we need to do some excavating and attain full exposure in order to gain closure.

Fortunately, once I identified the problem and began to deal with it, God lined up all the assistance I needed without delay. Everyone I engaged was immediately available, despite long waiting lists, and they did an exemplary job. Jackie and I didn't work out, but perhaps her purpose in my life was to facilitate the remodeling of my basement. In any case, it's now one of the coziest rooms of the house and my favorite place to hang out.

And the boat? Well, the next year I went to Exuma, the year after the shipwreck, my newly gained confidence had been shaken. I started looking for those winds again, so I wouldn't have to go boating. Lying in bed in the morning, looking for the whitecaps to tell me the water was too choppy to go boating, it occurred to me that while God had blessed me with a boat, the Thank You Lord, I was too vain to appreciate the blessing. Really, Melanie, are you going to let Satan or your own vanity steal your joy? I got up and got my gear together. During the entire ride to town, I kept telling myself, "I am a child of the most high God, and I am highly favored." I pulled my boat out of the dock with pride, not pride in myself, but in my Father, who loves me so much and blesses me so richly in everything. Remember, when I wrote about the Aberes? Perfect love casts out fear. My Father's love for me cast out my fear. It no longer mattered what the other boaters thought.

Since then, I have had many wonder-filled times on my boat, fishing and snorkeling. I have had dolphins swim up to me and invite me to play with them. Of course, I was petrified. When I was alone in the water, they caught me quite by surprise, and they are big up close. Vernal was on the boat, but I wasn't sure he could even see me, much less the dolphin. As one dolphin rolled over to expose his belly, I assumed for me to pet it, I was tempted to touch him, but then I was afraid I might spook him. Can't afford to pull back a nub. It's hard enough trying to find a girlfriend with two hands, let alone one, so I declined his invitation. It then occurred to me, suppose they decide to drag me off into the deep to show off their new friend to their mom? I took a few photos and swam toward the boat. I'll be braver next time.

Nowadays, I have no shortage of guys to hang out with. We go fishing and they captain the boat. Some of them dock even worse than I do. I've discovered that I'd much rather co-captain, sit back and enjoy the ride, snorkel, and fish. I don't mind not being in charge. I can defer to the knowledge and experience of another. In fact, I like it. I love having a man on board and in charge, of the boat, that is.

RELATIONSHIPS

Now, don't get the wrong impression, I wasn't totally asocial all those years upstate. I joined a few volunteer organizations, and I even became a Rotarian, but nothing seemed to fit. I didn't feel as if I was making any kind of significant difference in all my voluntary endeavors. The dating scene was non-existent, so I eventually joined a dating website.

The possibilities seemed endless. Page after page of women looking for love, and at least one on each page seemed reasonably appealing. When I initially joined, I didn't post a photo. I was much too fine and had it all going on, as they say, so I didn't want to be bombarded with a bunch of women whom I would have to end up rejecting. Vain much? Sometimes I boggle my own mind. Shockingly, I did not get one hit nor did anyone respond to my inquiries.

After about a year, I decided maybe I should post a photo and handle that mad rush of hits the best I could. My profile was conservative. I didn't boast about my beach house or boat or anything like that. I got a couple of inquiries from twenty-year olds in Russia and others from big, country dykes in Arkansas and the like. I got very few positive responses from the women I solicited—attractive, professional, feminine women. That was a blow to the old ego. Don't they know who I am? Much later in the game I surmised what the problem was. Many of the attractive, professional, feminine women were for the most part still in the closet, so they, too, were looking for mostly feminine women. Ironically, it seemed I was too masculine for the feminine women, but the really masculine women perceived me as feminine. At times, this whole gender thing can get a bit confusing. I know what my fellow Christians are saying right now, "God is not the author of confusion," a point well taken.

Anyway, I made a few acquaintances and went on some dates. I was introduced to the gay scene in Albany, which seemed to have promise, but that soon proved to be barren soil. The endless possibilities online became more and more scant. However, I did meet a couple of women with whom I established new friendships. My social life had grown, so the dating website served some purpose.

I went to a dance a few years ago given by SAGE, a gay organization that assists elderly gays and hosts fund-raising dances in Manhattan a couple of times a year. It was another tea dance, which was great, as my days of partying until the wee hours had long since passed, and it was a treat because there are surprisingly few clubs for mature lesbians to gather and dance in New York City. I was excited because there is usually a nice crowd of women. My cousin met me at the party. We hung out, had a few drinks and danced with some ladies. She was showing me the ropes again, as I had not been on the scene since my relationship with Maria, almost twenty years prior. We were having a good time, even though I hadn't met the love of my life. That was just as well. I probably wouldn't have known how to approach her anyway. I had been out of the game way too long and I had no rap.

My cousin and I were having our last drink, as the dance was ending, when I noticed a woman with a cane. She had to be about seventy, walking around the room, doing that all too familiar last cruise of desperation, looking for "the one," or *anyone*. A chill ran down my spine as I flashed back to when I was twenty. I remembered partying at Bonnie & Clyde's and seeing a woman about fifty come in the club alone. I felt such pity for her, and I thought, "Wow, I'll never be fifty and in the club, looking for love." And here I sat, fifty-five and in the club. Terrified, I silently screamed, "Oh, God, please don't let me be seventy and in the club, still searching!" The ride home was very depressing.

Returning to the dating website, I wasn't as discriminating as I had been in the past. It seems the older we get, the more jaded we become, especially women, particularly gay women. But I continued to date and be hopeful. I enjoyed dating and meeting new people. I love romance and the anticipation of a first kiss. I had resolved myself to dating until I was sure I met the right one. I could no longer afford to have a five-year relationship here or a three-year relationship there. No more rush to commitment, as had been the case in the past. I had given up my freedom way too quickly and inappropriately during my relationship with Samantha. I won't make that mistake again. Also, I was in my mid-fifties and knew my good looks didn't have too many decades left.

Last year, I went to another SAGE dance to meet up with someone I had met on-line and had dinner with the month before. Although there didn't seem to be any chemistry between us, she was a nice lady and could potentially be a friend, if nothing else. There was a good crowd, ladies ranging in age from their twenties to their eighties. The music was pumping and I was having a blast of a weekend. The night before I had attended a family wedding and was still in full party mode.

I was sitting at a booth with Megan and some of her friends. There was an eighty-something Black woman sitting next to me, and beside her, a younger Hispanic woman. The older woman told me how she had fallen a couple of years back and was in a nursing home for a while, but now she was recuperating at home. She seemed like a very sweet lady, and we had a pleasant conversation. (No, I haven't become that indiscriminate yet, hitting on an eighty-year-old, c'mon.) Anyway, a younger Black woman, my age, gestured that she wanted to sit next to the older lady, so I accommodated her. We then began to engage in conversation, and she told me that the older woman was her mother.

"That's so cool, you brought your mother to a lesbian dance with you," I said.

She laughed, "Oh, my mother is a lesbian, too."

"*Really!* Was moms trying to hit on me?" I joked, and we both laughed. "Is she your partner?" I asked, gesturing toward the Hispanic woman.

"No," she responded. "She's my mother's home health aide." She then explained how her mother had fallen and injured herself, "My mother had been with her partner for forty years. She's eighty-five. Two years ago her partner decided to leave her for some seventy-year-old who she met in the church, no less."

"What!" I nearly fell out of my seat.

"Yeah, after that my mom had a stroke and ended up in a nursing home."

"That's unbelievable. Do eighty-year-olds still have that much libido that they're pursuing hot chicks in their seventies?" I was flabbergasted.

"Apparently so. The good news is, the seventy-year-old left her after she used up all her money," she said with a smirk.

"And elderly people are still playing games like that?" I guess I am naive. So, you're not even safely in a committed relationship when you're eighty, eh? What a disappointment.

I pondered that conversation for many a day afterward. It was almost inconceivable to me that someone would do that—leave a forty-year relationship at the age of eighty for someone else. I mean, how much longer do you have to live that you can't stay with your companion of forty years for a few more? Even if you had a fling on the side, who would really care at that stage of the game? Or, if she had been unhappy in the relationship all along, why wait forty years to leave, or thirty or even twenty? I realize that we sometimes have difficulty walking away from a relationship for whatever reasons—we don't want to hurt the other party, don't want to be alone, or are comfortable, lazy, broke—but *damn*. That must have been some kind of hot seventy-year-old.

Then, I got a revelation. In any relationship, someone is eventually going to leave. Whether they walk, run, fly, or die, inevitably the relationship is going to come to an end. Nothing is forever. Each day, I grow to accept this more and more. I am beginning to perceive relationships in a whole new light. Instead of seeking forever from someone, I am learning to just appreciate whenever, however, wherever, whomever. No, I am not running around, whoring around. That is absolutely not what I mean. I mean, just *love*. Loving myself and being the best *me* that I can be—doing my best, giving my best, loving others and cherishing the love I get, from whomever: be it my sister, my best friend, a lover, or a smiling stranger passing by.

We waste so much time. We fail to honor so much love, taking for granted that it, he, or she will be there forever. And they never are. How I wish I had held my mother while she lay on her deathbed. How I regret not untying my brother, granting his last request of me. How much time have I consumed on worthless pursuits, trying to satisfy selfish, foolish desires? And now, I'm running out of time, and I'm running out of the people whom I love.

If I knew then what I know now, right, famous last words. Know this! Your days are numbered. Psalm 90:12 states, "Teach us to number our days that we may gain a heart of wisdom," which I call a loving heart, an appreciative heart. I tell you this truly and honestly. These days I pray to God to let me love Him more and more, just as He has loved me and will eternally. I strive to attain true agape love for people. And yes, I still want some eros, still want to share time with "the one" here on earth for however long it may last. But I ain't gonna settle. A couple of years ago, Samantha posted on my Facebook page something about how I don't appreciate my own value. She was probably right. But like Hollis, my stepfather, so aptly stated, "That used to be." From now on I only have time to give to people who value me, and my time. I want to be where I'm celebrated, not tolerated. And I will not force-feed someone who does not want to partake of my feast. If that means that I won't have "the one" here on earth, then so be it. God's will be done.

A friend of mine once gave me a book, *The Way to Love*, by Anthony De Mello. The basic premise of the book is not to get too attached to anyone or anything. That attachment is misery and limiting. He used the metaphor of listening to an orchestra but only focusing on the drum. If all you hear is the drum, you miss the beauty of all the rest of the instruments. I don't think he was proposing promiscuity but rather that universal, agape love I was talking about before. It's a wonderful ideal, but the Bible also tells us, "two is better than one." And God does want us to be in relationship, edifying relationships.

I don't know, perhaps I'm becoming jaded in my old age, too. On one hand, I do very much want a partner—a wife. This is the one thing I've longed for most of my life, "a love of my own." In pursuit of love, I've searched the streets and the clubs, high and low; I've shared many a bed; broken many a heart; and have had my heart broken more than I care to recount. In reality though, I knew nothing about love. I was futilely seeking something I was denied as a child and that I could never recover as an adult.

I have been self-involved most of my life. Yes, I could justify my behavior and say it was because I was neglected as a child. I could rationalize that because my emotional needs were not met as a child, I became overly preoccupied with my emotional needs as an adult, and as a result, I had a decreased ability to acknowledge the needs, talents, and very existence of others, on some levels. And true as this may be, it's no longer acceptable. This became very clear the day God told me, "Melanie, the world is not just a stage to your own personal drama." That was painful to hear, but when I thought about it, I saw that was exactly how I had been behaving. I have always been generous and have always been there when I was needed. I was a good daughter, sister, aunt, friend, lover. But in the end, it was somehow always about me.

First Corinthians 1:27 states, "But God chose the foolish things of the world to confound the wise." Remember the ten long years it took me to get over Samantha, even though I knew from the beginning it was not to be, even though I had just come out of a relationship and was ecstatic to be free, even though she was married, even though she was not really my type, even though we hardly spent any time together, even though I made an utter fool of myself pursuing this relationship, and even though everyone was tired of hearing me cry the blues, including me. Still, it took ten years to let it go. It blew my mind, yet much to my chagrin, I couldn't get free. It was not until I prayed and pleaded with God to free me that He could show me the one I really needed to be free of. God showed me that the key to my freedom was to be free of myself. I was so willful, so haughty. That was the lesson of the boat. I was the key: my pride and haughty eyes.

So now, when I think about it, as I date, I am really in no rush to get married. First, I think I would like to experience the whole orchestra. Again, I'm not advocating promiscuity.

Truth be told, there are very few people to whom I am attracted enough, to even want to kiss. But this time, I'm really in no rush to get committed. Now that I know how to love truly, and I know how valuable my love is, I want to have a relationship that is worthy. I accept it won't be forever, but I want it to be the ultimate, for whatever time we have together.

In the meantime, I just want to enjoy my life and the people in it. I got a lot of love to give, and it's my blessing and privilege to share it. Glory to God. It occurs to me, it was exactly ten years ago in 2003 when I was here in the Bahamas relishing my new-found freedom and anticipating the excitement of dating again. And now, here I am ten years later. Here we go again.

MEANDERINGS

"Wisdom is supreme; therefore get wisdom. And in all your getting, get understanding. Esteem her and she will exalt you; embrace her and she will honor you," (Proverbs 4:7-8). When I walk the beach, it amazes me how each wave touching the shore, transforms it in some way. From second to second, the beach changes with even the gentlest coaxing of the wind, like life, dynamic, no one moment ever occurring again. I enjoy photography, taking photos and capturing the moment. I learned early on that if you don't get the photo at that very second, you will never get the opportunity for that particular photo ever again. And do you know, I remember the images, the photos I missed, more vividly than the ones I have taken.

The beach breathes. The tide comes in and goes out again. Sometimes it may bring with it a beautiful piece of coral or a perfect, unbroken shell. Usually the coral only gets washed ashore after the waters have been very turbulent and have displaced it from its home. Most times, the waves bring debris, kind of like life in its ebb and flow. I mean, most of our days are "just another day," with its trials, annoyances, and responsibilities. Most days of an average life are not usually described as beautiful or wonderful, they're ordinary times we take for granted, and it's only the rarest days, indeed, that we feel gifted with something special to appreciate. Wouldn't it be marvelous, though, if we could find at least one thing beautiful or special in each of our few days here on earth. I'm just saying...

Living on a small island has helped me develop great patience. I often get the impression from my travels here and there that Americans are generally regarded by others around the world as impatient, indulgent, and rude. These characteristics are attributed even more so to New Yorkers. Now I admit, I've been known to go there in the past, but I have quickly discovered how imprudent those attitudes can be, especially on a small island.

For instance, we have all the comforts of home here on the island: telephone service, electricity, even internet. The services may be slower and less reliable, but they're available. Right now, as I sit here typing, my internet is out. It had been acting up all week, and then it just died. This happens a couple of times a month. There is typically one service guy who takes care of this side of the island. We have established a little rapport, and I tease him about the phone lines, "Yeah, man, I know you only got a few good working lines out here on the main frame, so when someone complains about their service, you just bump someone else from a good line and connect the one who's complaining. Pleeease....keep me on a good line!" He just smiles, but I know I'm right.

Last week I saw the phone truck go by my house, but our regular guy was on vacation. That's when my line started acting up. They bumped me off the good line! Yesterday, when it died completely, I called my friend Marilyn at the phone company. She was on vacation, too. A month ago, when I first returned to the island, I inquired about their new internet system. I think it's called the Wi-Max, and it connects directly with the satellite so you don't have to depend on the phone lines. Marilyn told me she would order one for me, but it may take a while as there is a shortage of them on the island because everyone wants one. When I spoke with Marilyn yesterday about the phone and the Wi-Max (not knowing she was on vacation), she said, "You mean you don't have the Wi-Max yet? They told me that they installed it weeks ago. I hope they didn't make a mistake and install it in someone else's house. Let me call and check on this for you right away, and I'll call you back."

She called about an hour later and explained, "Yes I spoke with Mr. Baxter, they're going to put the matter under investigation." I just sighed to myself and thought, you ain't gettin' no Wi-Max this trip. "Okay sweetie, thank you," was my reply. I went into town later that afternoon and stopped by the phone company to put some minutes on my cell phone. I figured I would inquire about the line repairs. It had not been officially reported, so I made out a report. The young woman took all my information and entered it into the computer. I asked how long it would take to be repaired. She smiled and said, "two to ten business days." Okey, dokey then.

I proceeded with my business about town, and on the way home I passed the phone repair truck on its way back to town. I made an abrupt U-turn and followed it back to the administrative office. As I got out of my car, there were three guys sitting out front. The guy in the truck was not my regular repairman, so I introduced myself and told him my plight.

He said, "Oh, man, we was just out there."

"Today?" I disappointedly asked.

"Nah, last week."

Yeah, that's when you messed me up, I thought. "So when you comin' back out east?"

He picked up his phone to check something. "Tomorrow we have an installation, then we go to Hooper's Bay" (totally in the opposite direction of my house).

"Oh, so that means you're not coming out east."

He just replied, "You ain't even in the system yet. Every morning I get a printout of my jobs for the day; if you're not in the system, you're not on the list."

"But I reported it just this afternoon. I saw the girl key it into the computer."

"Dem girls in the office lie, you know," was his reply.

Puzzled, I asked, "But why would she lie about that?" I never had any problems with anyone in the office, or any of the repairmen for that matter. In fact, I had always been rather impressed with the service and efficiency of the personnel.

"I don't know, but you need to go back down and report it again, and this time get her name, and let her show you the report in the computer."

Unbelievable. Now, I had to laugh. I thought I'd try a different avenue, "So, look, do you know anything about the Wi-Max?"

"That the Wi-Max man over dere," he said as he pointed to the guys sitting out front. I went over to them, smiling and proceeded to play "what's my line" to find out who the Wi-Max man was. After one wrong guess, no one was volunteering any information, and I didn't want to play anymore. I explained to them that Marilyn had spoken to Mr. Baxter this morning regarding the installation of my Wi-Max unit.

"I'm Mr. Baxter," one of them finally said, "I ain't spoke to Marilyn since last week." He wasn't smiling.

"See, I told you dem girls lie," the other one piped in.

Long story short, Mr. Baxter made an appointment with me to be here today, Thursday, between 9 a.m. and 1 p.m. It is now 5 p.m. No Mr. Baxter yet, but I'm cool.

When my resources are limited, I find I'm more creative. If I want to get on line tonight, I'll just cruise around the neighborhood until I pick up a signal. I will try to reach Mr.

Baxter tomorrow to let him know that I took him at his word and try to guilt him into getting out here. By Monday (They don't typically work on week-ends, so I only have tomorrow.) if my internet is not on, I will be a bit disappointed and probably a bit more aggressive. But in the meantime, why get bent out of shape? It is what it is.

Yes, I will do whatever I can to accomplish my goal, but in the meantime, the in-between time, I just have to accept how things are until they are different. Being angry or anxious is not going to get my internet reconnected any faster. It will only make my blood pressure go up, spoil my beautiful day, and cause me to make enemies at the phone company. Mr. Baxter did come Saturday morning to install my Wi-Max. We watched a sermon together while he was doing the installation, and I made a new friend at the phone company.

As I reflect back on my life, on the things I can actually remember after years of methodically attempting to block things out, it has become so clear how everything and everyone has had a part in making me who I am. The journey is one continual learning experience, a process of evolution. There is an old saying: "No man is my enemy, no man is my friend, every man is my teacher." As I have previously stated, it was all a set-up.

From the very beginning, the unfolding of events and people in my life, was all planned to bring me here. The process begins from our childhood, from the womb actually, if you consider genetics. But for now, let's just consider our experiences. If my mother, father, stepfather, grandmother, grandfather, etc. had not been who they were, I would not be who I am. I might have been more passive, had my mother been more aggressive. I might have been straight if I had more of a positive father figure, but I am who I am for a reason.

When I think of shooting dope at the age of thirteen, how

horrifying. Yet it probably would have been more horrifying and devastating had I done it at a later age. I could have contracted HIV instead of hepatitis C. I could have ended up on the methadone program and been relegated to a lifetime of drug addiction. What were they thinking when they came up with that program?

Did I mention that I got fired from my first physical therapy job? I was working at a Brooklyn Hospital. The chief physical therapist was an attractive Black woman around my age. We began hanging out, seeing each other, and sleeping together. Karen informed me that she was also dating our department head, Dr. Lebowitz, a seventy-year-old unattractive Jewish man who used to drive a green Jaguar. When she told me she was dating him I asked, "Well where's *your* Jag?"

She laughed and said, "I wish."

"Then I know you got some minks, big bank account, something, right?"

"Well, we go out for nice meals, and he gives me some money from time to time."

"What, do you love him?"

"Aw, come on, Mel," she answered.

Now, I wasn't in love with Karen, but I hated to see any woman being taken advantage of. Karen worked hard at the hospital, and I didn't see her getting any special favor. "A nice meal, you need to be getting way more than that. The man is over seventy, and you're only twenty-seven. What are you doing?" Well, my words must have sunk in after a while, 'cause old Dr. Lebowitz got mighty hostile towards me, and I towards him (subtly and professionally, of course). He fired me.

At first, I was upset and angry and wanted to sue for discrimination (my being gay). I contacted the Civil Liberties Union, but they said I didn't have much of a case. This was back in the late seventies. I got over it quickly enough, and instead, I decided to enjoy the break. So I applied for unemployment and food stamps and had a marvelous time in my East Village apartment. The nights I wasn't out partying, I was home smoking herb and eating Haagen Daas ice cream by the pints. At twenty, I could do that and it wouldn't even show. Now, if I get Haagen Daas once a year, it's a treat, and that pint goes a long way. I figured I worked hard these past years, working and going to school, so I deserved a six-month break. It was fabulous! But after six months of unemployment and food stamps, I went back to work, refreshed and ready to conquer the world. That was when I met John and Sam, the rehab contractors, and started amassing my fortune. So my getting fired was actually a blessing in disguise.

I wasn't concerned with much then except making money and having fun. I wasn't going to any church or even seeking God with any conviction. In fact, I even became a Buddhist for a minute. It was not so much a religious decision as it was a social decision. You see, Buddhism became quite popular amongst the lesbians back in the late seventies, and where the fine women were, that's where I wanted to be. So, after joining the temple some of my new friends and I went back to my apartment to construct an altar. We had a wooden box in which we placed my Gohonzon, a scroll with Chinese and Sanskrit characters. There was also supposed to be some live greenery and water on the altar, but I don't remember the whole construct.

Each day, you were to kneel in front of your altar and chant, "Nam myoho renge kyo," which I did devotedly for at least a few weeks. I have always been open-minded regarding religion and philosophy, and I still am. But I gotta tell you, one night I was awakened by this fat spirit in black and white plaid trousers, rapidly waddling from the living room where my altar was towards me in my bedroom. No, it wasn't

Buddha. I couldn't get the Lord's Prayer out of my mouth fast enough until he was gone.

All right, as vivid and real as it was, I figured maybe I just had too much herb and Haagen Daas, so although I was shaken up, I dismissed it, but notice, I never forgot it. Days after, I was visited by the floating head of an old woman, pulling down on one of her eyes, and travelling the same path as the fat man. I was so frightened (my head was off the pillow), I could barely utter the Lord's Prayer, but I did get it out. She floated off into the wall. I was sitting straight up by this time, and no, I wasn't taking LSD back then. The next morning, I took down my altar, brought my Gohonzon into the kitchen, held it over the tub, and burned it. Sorry Buddhists, no offense, but my spirit indicated to me that I was idol worshipping. I did ask for God's forgiveness, and those visitations stopped.

Although I wasn't attending church during this time period, I did pray, maybe not everyday, but I was aware of God. And He was leading me and protecting me all this time, unbeknownst to me, probably, because I had praying grandparents. Mama and Papa were definitely in relationship with the Lord. So I'm sure their prayers were covering me, and for most of my youth, I gave them plenty to pray about. But I didn't really start seeking the Lord, until after my mother's death, when I began to know that I needed serious help.

Oh, and my spirit visits returned after Mommy died. She came to me. She was kneeling in the corner of my bedroom praying, I assume for me. I just realized this very moment that she was letting me know that she loved and forgave me and probably wanted my forgiveness, too. At the time, though, her presence frightened me, and I tried praying her away. I later regretted missing once again, the opportunity to say good-bye and to tell her how much I loved her. I believe she knows.

Anyway, it was shortly after Mommy's visit that I started reading my Bible more and attending various churches, seeking a church in which I felt comfortable and spiritually fed. I wasn't quite sure what to look for in a church and I didn't really know anything back then about being spiritually fed. There was just something in me, telling me I needed to know God better.

You know, when you begin to get into relationship with God, more and more, He shows you how much He loves you and how He is always there for you, always right on time. The other day, I was discussing my book with my best friend, working on the final chapters, trying to sum things up, and put everything together. She recommended a book by Florence Scovel Shinn, *The Game of Life and How to Play It*. This was such a blessing in reiterating and reconfirming lessons and truths that God has been teaching me along the way.

When asked by one of her students about the darkness before the dawn, Florence replied, "Before the big demonstration everything seems to go wrong and deep depression clouds the consciousness. It means that out of the subconscious are rising the doubts and fears of the ages. These old derelicts of the subconscious rise to the surface, to be put out." Isn't that almost exactly how I described it in the beginning of the book? That's when my spiritual battle began. That's when I began to seriously pray and seek the Lord. Remember when I needed help giving up cocaine and started attending the Catholic Church? The game was afoot.

Then God sent me off to the wilderness. After all the deaths and losses, I lost my job and began to lose my mind. I had to be alone, with Him. I didn't know that's what He intended at the time, but I was compelled into the wilderness. Initially it was exciting: a new house in the country, decorating, seeing the wildlife. Also, my relationship with Maria continued for seven years after relocating upstate, so I was only there part-time and in the city the remainder of the time. But even then, there was an incredible loneliness. Most times when I was leaving the city to go back to the wilderness, I would begin to cry about halfway there. Sometimes I'd put on "The Long and Winding Road" by the Beatles because my road home was long and winding, then I'd really sob (I know—crybaby). I just felt so isolated, yet I couldn't leave. My cousin jokingly said one day, "Well, at least no one can tell you they were in the neighborhood and just decided to drop by." I was having a wilderness experience, and after Maria and I broke up, my solitude was undeniable.

With few exceptions, the great names of the Bible were wilderness people. Right after Jesus was baptized, a voice from heaven said, "You are my son whom I love; with you I am well pleased. At once the Spirit sent him out into the desert and he was in the desert forty days, being tempted by Satan. He was with wild animals and angels attended him" (Mark 1:11-12).

In Biblical terms, the wilderness is always a place of both physical and spiritual journeying and discovery. Abraham wandered there for more than half his life, and this is where he learned obedience to the will of God. Moses wandered in the wilderness during the latter years of his life to discover much of the power of God, and he became the appointed vessel of the Lord's will for the people of his day and generations to follow.

The wilderness provides a cloister where the deeper things of God and life can be pursued and practiced. It is a place of discovery: a place from which to emerge in order to fulfill God's assignments and a place to revisit for further contemplation and communion with the Divine. Jesus often returned to the wilderness when He needed spiritual renewal.

I'm not comparing myself to these Biblical greats,

although, aside from Jesus, they all had flaws, but I do recognize now that God led me into the wilderness for a purpose.

NEVER ALONE

For so many years of my life I sought love. I prayed to God to send me someone to love, someone of my very own. I prayed for other things as well. In later years I prayed for Him to use me, to show me my purpose in life. But for so many years it seemed my primary goal in life was to love and be loved and belong to someone and to feel that I was important to someone, that I came first, that I mattered. When it began to seem as though I would never attain that special love, I became a bit frustrated and maybe even a little angry with God. I began to tell Him, "If you're not going to give me someone of my own, then don't make me want it so badly!" But, even though I wasn't getting what I thought I most wanted, I remained in relationship with Him, ever seeking His face. God was blessing me in so many ways and teaching me what true love really is.

Jesus tells us in Matthew 6:25, "Therefore I tell you, do not worry about your life, what you will eat or drink; or about your body, what you will wear. Is not life more important than food and the body more important than clothes....Who by worrying can add a single hour to his life? ...So do not worry, saying, what shall we eat or what shall we drink or what shall we wear? For the Pagans run after these things and your Heavenly Father knows that you need them. But seek first His kingdom and His righteousness, and all these things will be given to you as well." Recently, I have begun to study teachings on Jesus's love for us, for me. I have begun to ask Him to let me intimately know His love for me and to love Him intimately in return.

For years, the winters that I spent at my beach house were some of the loneliest times of my life. You see, on the beach most people are coupled. All my neighbors are my age or older, married couples with children and grandchildren. The tourists are usually coupled as well. Even most of the natives on the island are married. So my aloneness became particularly acute on the beach. One year, there were even two stray dogs that seemed to be a couple. They would come right on my beach, right in front of my house and bathe together, play together and look out for one another. All I could do was look up to the sky and say, "Really Lord, you're kidding, right? Even the dogs have mates."

The Doggie Duo Playing on my beach

But now, the loneliness is not so ever present. I don't scream and cry and beg for that "someone." I am becoming more intimately entwined with Jesus, and it is truly a wonderful thing. No, I'm not floating around on a cloud, holier than thou. To keep it real, since I've been in the Bahamas during this winter of 2013, I have had erotic dreams almost every night. Perhaps it is something about the crashing of the waves, or the half-naked bodies on the beach, or maybe it was a kiss I got just before I left New York. I prayed about it because I've never experienced erotic dreams every night, so I wanted to make sure some succubus wasn't hanging around.

More than likely, I am filled with anticipation about a lot of things, and it's getting me excited in many ways, which is manifested in my dreams as sexual excitement. This makes sense. My point is, I have begun to be blessed with a deeper relationship with the Lord, and it is a joyful and peaceful experience. And I know now that I was *never* alone, not for a moment; that He was always with me, waiting for me, as He is waiting for you. He is already a part of you. He is the very love in you, waiting to manifest and evolve. When asked what is the greatest commandment, Jesus answered, "Love the Lord your God with all your heart and with all your soul and with all your mind and with all your strength. The second is this: Love your neighbor as yourself" (Mark 12:30). God wants us to love ourselves and appreciate our lives. He wants us to be all that we can be, for His glory and for our joy. Please understand that your relationship with God is a very personal thing, and no one can tell you how you should worship or what is right or wrong for you. No one that is, except God. And if you seek Him and open your heart to receive Him, He will guide you.

I mentioned that I currently belong to a Pentecostal church, because when I first started attending, there was an anointing for me there. This past year I have not been attending as regularly. My last visit was quite hurtful and disappointing. Our pastor, the same pastor through whom I felt God was speaking to me, preached a very homophobic sermon. He began by addressing the youth of the congregation, telling them not to be influenced by what they see in the media, and that just because something is a law, that doesn't make it right. He then spoke about how when Christians try to express their religion it can be considered a hate crime. What! Hate crime connotes an act of violence. Was he advocating that violence against a person was acceptable? Was I hearing correctly, or was he just having a bad day?

Perhaps the church board encouraged him to be more militant in his teaching. I don't know, but he sure fell a few pegs in my eyes that day. I anticipate, when my book is published and becomes as widely read as I pray it will be, that I will be asked to leave the church, and it will be okay. Or maybe they will begin to see things in a new light and become more loving. I purposely didn't use the word *tolerant* because I think we need to go further than that. But if my church no longer welcomes me, so be it. I belong to The Lord, not to the church. This past year my spirit has been suggesting to me that it's time for a change, anyway.

Recently, I heard a minister speak about Anne Rice, a world famous author, who was at one time an atheist. As he told it, over ten years ago she converted to Christianity, but then in July of 2010 she posted the following on her Facebook page: "Today I quit being a Christian. I'm out. I remain committed to Christ as always but not to being 'Christian' or to being part of Christianity. It's simply impossible for me to 'belong' to this quarrelsome, hostile, disputatious, and deservedly infamous group. For ten years, I've tried. I've failed. I'm an outsider. My conscience will allow nothing else. My faith in Christ is central to my life. My conversion from a pessimistic atheist lost in a world I didn't understand, to an optimistic believer in a universe created and sustained by a loving God is crucial to me. But following Christ does not mean following His followers." Kudos to you, Anne. It's all about relationship, not religion. So don't you ever let anyone deter you from getting to know our Father. He knows and loves you, and He wants nothing more than for you to come to know and love Him.

You younger folks are searching. Your souls are hungry for direction, for the answer, right? Begin with the Bible, please, or at least include it in your search. I know, it's so old, and it's been so "done," but it's so full of wisdom. If you just try it, with an open mind and heart, The Bible will speak to you. Maybe not right away. Your intellect may try to get in the way, but give God a chance. Download the Bible to your iPad or your smart phone, perhaps that will make it more current for you. Be aware of what the Bible refers to as false prophets and idols, like pop stars, fashion and popularity. Don't let others determine your value. You are a Child of God. Most of your friends on Facebook don't even know who you really are. "Above all else, guard your heart, for out of it flow the issues of life" (Proverbs 4:23). Please don't think I'm being judgmental. I know that God is using me not because of who and what I am, but rather, in spite of who and what I am.

Remember the apostle Paul? He wrote these words from prison during his crusade to bring Christ to the Gentiles.

> Not that I have already attained all this or have already been made perfect, but I press on to take hold of that for which Christ Jesus took hold of me. Brothers, I do not consider myself yet to have taken hold of it. But one thing I do: Forgetting what is behind and straining toward

> what is ahead, I press on toward the goal to win the prize for which God has called me heavenward in Christ Jesus. All of us who are mature should take such a view of things. And if on some point you think differently, that, too, God will make clear to you. Only let us live up to what we have already attained (Phillipians 3:12).

I like to put that last sentence in street vernacular: "Act, like you know." We all start out some place, all on different levels of our development. So let us grow where we are planted, but, let us be determined to grow.

My journey is just beginning. I pray that I have many miles to go before I sleep. God has begun to show me my purpose, and I am so very thankful that he has allowed me to live long enough to get some wisdom and some peace. My mother gave me a trinket once that I carry with me to this day. It is one of my most precious possessions. There used to be a cigarette brand specifically marketed to women called Virginia Slims. The theme song to their TV commercial went like this: "You've come a long way baby, to get where you got to today. You got your own cigarette now baby, you've come a long, long way." Oh, the tobacco companies, gotta love 'em. Anyway, Mommy was smoking Virginia Slims at the time, and as a promotional item they attached a brass key chain to the pack with the slogan, "You've come a long way, baby." That key chain held the keys to my then apartment in the Bronx, and now it holds the keys to all my mortgage-free homes. Yes, Mommy, I have come a long way, baby!

I pray that those of you who don't know Our Father yet will begin to develop a desire to get to know him. Those of you who do know Him, maybe it's time to get to know Him even better. Again, I'm not judging. Who am I to judge? I've shared some of my humanity with you. You know I'm a work in progress. Accordingly, I will not allow you to judge me. To again quote Paul, "I care very little if I am judged by you or by any human court. Indeed, I do not even judge myself. My conscience is clear, but that does not make me innocent" (1 Corinthians 4:3).

I sometimes ponder why as we get older, our eyes tend to get weaker. Or is it that we just grow weary of seeing the hurt, the indifference, and the greed? Why should so many be in need when God has given us enough for everyone? At the very least, no one should be dying of thirst or hunger. It amazes me how after all the thousands of years that man has been on this earth, our collective spirits seemed not to have evolved much at all.

Thank you for allowing me to share some of my life stories with you, some of my laughter, some of my pain. I have tried to be as honest as possible, not so much so that you would know me, but so that you would know God's love and mercy for me, and for you. I am acutely aware that many of you have experienced much more pain and hardship than I could ever imagine. It breaks my heart to see how we hurt and exploit one another in so many horrific ways. Please know that fifty percent of the net proceeds of the sales of each book will be gratefully donated to charities promoting the welfare of children; some will be Christian based organizations, and some will be secular. We are our brothers' keeper.

Oh, and you'll be glad to know I have expanded my journey out of the wilderness. I'm better now, at least better than I was, and it's time to get back in the world. I got an apartment in the city, and I'm ready for new life lessons, new loves, and new adventures. I'll keep you posted. In the meantime, let's walk in love. Shalom, Salaam, Namaste my beloveds. See you in the city. Peace, I'm out!

ABOUT THE AUTHOR

Melanie E. Lewis, a God-made millionaire, humbly acknowledges- I may have implemented the plan, but it was divinely formulated.

A proud, lesbian woman of faith, LGBT activist, and native New Yorker, Melanie has made it a practice to live a benevolent life. Graduating Tuskegee Institute, Magna Cum Laude, she experienced a fulfilling and rewarding career as a self-employed Physical Therapist. She also explored other lucrative ventures including real estate investments. However, throughout her life she has always committed time and money to helping others.

Melanie has served on the board of Family Services Inc. of Poughkeepsie, participated in the Big Sisters program for many years, volunteered at the Poughkeepsie Children's Home, was a CASA volunteer, and is a Rotarian. Her primary concern has always been the safety and tutelage of children.

In keeping with her magnanimous nature she plans to donate fifty percent of all net proceeds of her book sales to charitable organizations promoting the welfare of children. We are our brothers' keeper.

Citizen of the world, she lives alternately between her homes in Upstate, New York, The Bahamas, and Harlem, New York.

www.ingramcontent.com/pod-product-compliance
Lightning Source LLC
Chambersburg PA
CBHW021123300426
44113CB00006B/266